MY WISDOM INSPIRED LIFE

A Provocative True Story

RICHARD HAASNOOT

Contact: haasnoot@cox.net

ISBN: 0615729215

ISBN 13:   9780615729213

Table of Contents

Dedication

This book is dedicated to Paramahansa Yogananda, my beloved guru, who guides my journey every day. His guidance is so deeply appreciated.

Special thanks are also given to Sogyal Rinpoche, Alice Bailey, and Djwhal Khul.

My family, both immediate and extended, deserves thanks for helping to bring the love into my life that made this book possible.

Note: Despite best efforts there are probably some typos still left in this. . . . . my apologies. . . .feel free to tell me of the more serious ones. Thank you!

ONE
CHAPTER

Wisdom....What is it?

Since the title of this book is *My Wisdom Inspired Life*, starting with a common understanding of what I mean by "wisdom" seems like it would be very helpful.

It turns out that "wisdom" is defined two very different ways.

The first way of defining the word is the way most people define it in our culture today. Very simply, if stated as a recipe, the definition looks like this:

> Start by becoming very knowledgeable.
> Add a dose of life experience.
> Add two doses of high-quality judgment.

Not surprisingly, this definition leads to some further conclusions. For example, because of the "life experience" element, we tend to think of wise people as older rather than younger. If you search images for "wise people," you find that most of the images are for people about 50 years of age and older. The first image from the search that comes up is for Albert

Einstein. This definition also suggests that you need to be well-educated, either formally in academic institutions or informally with high quality life experiences.

The dictionary supports this definition. For example, the Merriam Webster Dictionary says:

Definition of WISDOM

a) Accumulated philosophic or scientific learning : knowledge
b) Ability to discern inner qualities and relationships : insight
c) Good sense : judgment
d) Generally accepted belief (challenges what has become accepted *wisdom* among many historians — Robert Darnton)
e) A wise attitude, belief, or course of action
f) The teachings of the ancient wise men

As helpful as this definition is, it is not the definition of "wisdom" that I am using. Rather, appropriately enough, I am utilizing the definition that comes from multiple wisdom tradition teachings. I believe that this definition will eventually become the standard definition, but it requires some significant personal transformations before being broadly accepted.

First, some background is helpful. The wisdom traditions tell us that we have two minds, an upper mind and a lower mind. This can also be described as our knowledge and wisdom minds.

The lower mind is the capability where knowledge resides. We acquire knowledge through our five senses. As a result, knowledge comes from our external world.

In the lower mind, knowledge is managed by logic and emotions. This management has several goals including determining what knowledge is important and unimportant to us. We also want to know what knowledge is true and trusted and what knowledge is less reliable and even suspect. In the world of knowledge, the ultimate truth management tool is something like the scientific method. This method rigorously controls variables in an effort to determine truth.

Knowledge is a world of dualities. It is where good and bad, high and low, right and wrong, etc. exist. It falls to our logic and emotions to determine where specific pieces of knowledge fit. Not surprisingly, people often see the same knowledge in very different ways.

The wisdom traditions tell us that the upper or higher mind is the home of wisdom. Unlike knowledge that is acquired when our senses focus on the external world, we acquire wisdom through an inner focus. Intuition, which is the voice of our soul or that spark of divinity, is our portal to wisdom. Intuition exists in all of us, although it is largely dormant is most, occasionally active in some, and fully functional in very few people.

Unlike knowledge's world of dualities, the world of wisdom is one of absolute truths. As our intuition develops, the insights we gain take on a level of truth that is greater than our knowledge that $1 + 1 = 2$.

Some perspective from the 24 volumes of the Ageless Wisdom (more on this source later but it comes from an enlightened, great master) may help deepen this understanding of what wisdom is.

> "Wisdom has to do with the development of the life within the form, with the progress of the spirit through those ever-changing vehicles, and with the expansions of consciousness that succeed each other from life to life. It deals with the life side of evolution. Since it deals with the essence of things and not the things themselves, it is the intuitive apprehension of the truth apart from the reasoning facility, and the innate perception that can distinguish between the false and the true, between the real and the unreal."[1]

> "Wisdom is the science of the Spirit, just as knowledge is the science of matter. Knowledge is separatism and objective, whilst wisdom is synthetic and subjective. Knowledge divides; wisdom unites. Knowledge differentiates whilst wisdom blends."[2]

Accessing and developing wisdom requires an inner focus that is most often achieved through practices like meditation, contemplation, prayer, and chanting. While meditation is the most important of these practices, it is not the only way that we access intuition. People also have intuitive insights during moments of inner quietness or calmness. These can be times like watching a sunset, taking a shower, or running.

Since intuition is so critical to accessing wisdom, some better definitions of this keyword might help. Let's start with the dictionary definitions. They use phrases like "a quick and ready insight" and "the power or faculty of attaining to direct knowledge or cognition without evident rational thought and inference." Relative to the wisdom definitions, these are actually pretty helpful for our purposes in understanding wisdom.

Again from the wisdom traditions, specifically the Ageless Wisdom, here are a couple of quotes that hopefully advance understanding of this keyword.

"Intuition is the synthetic understanding which is the prerogative of the soul......"[3]

".......intuition is the source or the bestower of revelation. Through the intuition, progressive understanding of the ways of God in the world, and upon behalf of humanity are revealed; through the intuition, the transcendence and immanence of God is sequentially grasped;........through the intuition man arrives at the experience of the kingdom of God, and discovers the nature, the type of lives and of phenomena, and the characteristics of the Sons of God as they come into manifestation."[4]

"Intuition brings with its appearance three qualities: illumination, understanding and love."[5]

The wisdom traditions are very clear that intuition is the voice of our soul. Our soul is that spark of divinity that exists in all of us. As such, our intuition is a method God uses to communicate with us. The challenge for the vast majority of us is first paying attention to intuitive insights and then not misconstruing them through our ego's interpretation. Until a stronger connection to our intuition develops (for example, through a deep and regular meditation practice), we need to be a bit cautious because of the risk of misunderstanding an insight.

Yogananda makes the manifestation of wisdom clear when he says, "Discrimination born of intuition through soul contact insures right judgment in any given situation. The soul, through the agency of intuition, drops divine guidance into the consciousness of the devotee; intuitive guidance manifests as wisdom through the discriminative faculty to guide the intellect or reason to the right determination."

Intuition is pretty cool!

While this book utilizes the second definition of wisdom, the first definition is very real and practical for most people. In a way, the second definition of wisdom builds dramatically on the first definition. It provides a new and far more accurate set of insights to guide judgment.

I will talk more about this later, but there is one very significant and even startling difference between knowledge and wisdom. When we acquire new knowledge, our reaction is often, "wow, I did not know that." On the other hand, when we acquire new wisdom through our intuition, our reaction is "wow, I now remember." This is because wisdom has always been a part of who we are, but accessing it has not been especially easy.

Wisdom is also pretty cool!

The following chapters follow the ever so slow emergence of wisdom in my life through an awakening intuition, an intuition that was largely dormant until about 40 years into my life journey. While largely dormant in this period, there were flashes of intuition that frequently and power-fully changed my life. The source of these "flashes" was largely not under-stood at the time.

But, I'll let you see this for yourself as the story unfolds over the fol-lowing chapters.

TWO
CHAPTER

Intuition

Intuition spoke....I listened.

What I have heard is transforming my life for the good, the very good.

This is my story. Little did I know when this journey started where it would lead. Today I see it as a journey that brought greater happiness and wisdom to a life that had little of either. Be aware that if you allow me to take you on this journey, we'll go to places in the heart and mind that may seem to transcend and even sometimes confound logical analysis.

This is the story of the son of immigrant parents. Through their guidance and inspiration I set out to live the American dream. After some brief false starts, this meant embarking on a business career. For the longest time I thought climbing the corporate ladder would consume the rest of my productive life.

Then intuition spoke....this changed everything although when it first happened I was clueless about the changes that would ultimately unfold. Intuition's communication broke through my intense and rigorous logical approach to the world. I found myself making major life decisions that always went counter to every logical bone in my body. Yet, they have all proven to be the best decisions I ever made. Marriage, career, family, and my spiritual life have all been profoundly changed for the better with the unerring aid of intuition's communication.

For those of you who believe that humans are "hard wired" thus essentially making them prisoners who they are now and incapable of major change, please consider the following. First, neuroscience has repeatedly confirmed brain plasticity, which means that the brain is capable of profound change. Scientists know that we are not "hard wired." I know this from my personal journey where I have experienced the following profound changes, all for the good, in my life.

- Going from not believing in God to deeply knowing God through my intuition (goes well beyond just believing in God).
- Changing from a highly competitive person (would compete at most everything in life) to a highly collaborative person.
- Shifting from believing that maybe I did not know it all but what I did not know was not worth knowing to an extremely deep appreciation of my ignorance about so much in the world.
- Going from being just "satisfied" with life to actually experiencing real happiness with increasing frequency in my life.
- Changing from a very strong egocentric perspective to a much more compassionate experience of life and ultimately the desire to rid myself completely off egotism.

This story is not another *Conversations with God* book. That sort of experience appears to happen to a very, very few people.

Rather, the way intuition repeatedly spoke to me appears to be God's preferred and most frequent form of speaking to us humans. From all that I know now, He speaks to all of us in ways similar to what I experienced. I possess the same abilities you have. Yes, I eventually saw these abilities after being blind and ignorant to them for most of my life. You have them.....we all do. This book may help you to see these abilities.....if so, they could unlock wondrous insights capable of positively transforming your life. PLEASE *know* that you have everything you need right now to access the abilities and experiences I share in this book.

It is highly probable that you can look at your own life from a different perspective and be amazed at the interconnected experiences in your life. By seeing their patterns you will better understand where you have been and where you are probably headed.

In Steve Jobs' 2005 Stanford commencement speech, he talks about connecting the dots of your life. That is, looking back to see how an early event led to another and another. Sometimes that early or first event might have seemed trivial at the time, but as life unfolds its wonders, we see that a big event later in life probably would not have occurred without a previous series of apparently smaller events. In a way, this is a book about connecting the dots and seeing the guiding hand that led from one dot or even to another and another.

In connecting the dots a picture emerges. It depicts the purpose and themes of this lifetime. From this we acquire meaning that guides and accelerates the emergence of our purpose TODAY. Despite the ego's claim to supremacy, our life is God's doing. My puny ego could never have dreamed or orchestrated the life I now enjoy and marvel at.

As you'll see, our intuition speaks in ways currently unfamiliar to most of us....primarily because we do not look at certain life events as mediums through which He speaks. It's no surprise that many people are unaware that intuition speaks to them. I needed to develop a whole new understanding of methods of communication and "language."

Please think about important points as you consider the statement "intuition spoke." First, this is not an ego trip. There is absolutely nothing special about me. Nothing. Everyone reading this can have the same experience by following some rather simple steps.

Second, I know that my intuition spoke because the great masters and God realized beings reveal to us the ways that intuition communicates with all of us. Knowing the ways that intuition communicates with us makes it more likely that we will first recognize communication and then understand and interpret our intuition's interactions with us differently than we have in the past. Lastly, there is an "inner knowing" component to this communication....and all of us have the ability to develop it through rather simple methods.

The good news is that even with rather rudimentary skills most of us can be aware when our intuition speaks and understand our intuition's message for us. I possess no extraordinary or special abilities. In many ways, the opposite is true. As you'll see, it took a figurative two by four piece of lumber to my head for me to even start waking up. I was in the deep zone of a business career, thinking I knew it all....and giving my intuition and God no time or attention.

In part, what inspired me to write this book are basic messages of hope. Our intuition speaks to all of us. We are not alone. God wants to help us and God does help us if only we will "listen." With some effort virtually everyone can "hear." With the same effort, we can understand our intuition's message for us....and when we follow our intuition's advice life is good, easier, and happier.

If I can wake up, you can. Yes, my intuition spoke. I listened....and your intuition is speaking to you. You can listen, hear, learn, and transform your life for the good of yourself and others.

Do I really know that it is my intuition that spoke? Yes. I know with a level of certainty that is greater than my confidence that $1 + 1 = 2$. Am I sure it was my intuition and not something else? Yes.

Great questions.

I have no need or desire convince you of this. I will tell my story and you judge for yourself. More importantly, experience what I have experienced and then judge for yourself. Proof lies in the inner intuitive experience....not your logical mind.

THREE
CHAPTER

God

This is the most daunting chapter I can imagine ever attempting to write in my life. How do I write about something so beyond my ability to fully comprehend? What do I write?

I am not referring to a Christian, Hindu, or any other religion's particular God. I am referring to a universal God that appears in virtually every major wisdom tradition (Buddhism is somewhat of an exception but that is too extensive a topic for this book).

Let me start with some words about my intent. It is not my intent to offend anyone. It is not my intent to convince anyone that what I'm about to say is what you should believe. It is my intent to provide meaning and context for this book by describing my understanding of God.

Does God exist? There is a small percentage of our population that says "no" and "maybe." Based on Harris research 90% of Americans believe that God does exist. But this is not an effort to make a numerical case for God. No numbers will convince believers to not believe or nonbelievers to believe.

Does God exist? I answer this question with an enthusiastic "yes!" My reasons are fairly simple. I start by taking a look at the world around me with its mind-boggling complexity and believe this did not develop out of randomness or chaos. The world we live in exists with some very tight tolerances. If our body temperature changes just a few degrees we can die. If the planet's average temperature changes 2° in one year catastrophic events would result from this change. Please don't get tied up in the details of this. The message is simply that we live in an incredibly complex and amazing world that no single human or mass of humans could possibly create or re-create the world we live in. Go beyond our earth and stare into the skies at the vastness that surrounds us. The result is the same…awe at the wonders we can see…..and what about we cannot see?

I agree with one of the greatest quantum physicists of our time who concluded that our universe must have been created and exists today with the assistance of a "guiding hand"….that "guiding hand" is the hand of God.

Ultimately when we rely on external sources and observations as the basis for our belief in God, it is just that, a belief. It's only when we begin to develop our inner knowing….our intuition, that knowing God changes from a belief to a certainty. No amount of *knowledge* will ever produce an absolute, unqualified, certain knowing of God's existence.

Only wisdom can produce that level of certainty. Wisdom develops through our intuition.

While we all have intuitive ability, it is latent in the vast majority of human beings today. Despite this fact, many people believe they have intuitive ability because they confuse gut feelings and other sorts of feelings with intuition. Even when people have a true flash of intuition, that intuitive insight then gets filtered through our ego, values and beliefs. The result is that in many cases the substance and quality of the original intuitive insight changes dramatically. Despite these challenges evidence from the wisdom traditions suggest that intuitive ability is awakening in many more people. In the early awakening stages caution is appropriate when it comes to understanding an "intuitive insight." Regarding intuition, Paramahansa Yogananda says, "Human knowledge, no matter how proliferative, will always be limited without the wisdom (intuitive perception) of the soul, the singular revealer of the Creator." He adds that it is "...the faculty of intuition is through which one knows Ultimate Truth."

(Paramahansa Yogananda is a new name for most of you. For me, he is an avatar or God realized being and my deeply beloved guru for life. You will learn more, much more, about him as this book goes on.)

For people without a well-developed intuition, they rely on knowledge and logic to determine truth and believe that truth is very subjective. For them "Ultimate Truth" is not credible...understood....but there is an "Ultimate Truth" for all great mystics and sages. Another sage describes it as the "truth beyond all intellectual understanding."

"Ultimate Truth" is something that intellectual, knowledge and logic based people can begin to explore through study of these traditions from the perspective of their current paradigm. The great scholar Huston Smith is probably the single best source and place to begin this study. Exploring some of the works of leading quantum physicists can also provide the beginnings of a bridge from purely logical understanding of the world to an expanded intuitive understanding. This is a start....a sort of bridge for the logical mind to take. But developing intuition requires ultimately moving to the inner journey.

Yogananda goes on to say, "When this innate power of knowing is developed by calmness and meditation into the pure, unerring intuition of the soul, the devotee has access to the library of all wisdom contained right within himself...."

Having said that, please remember that the vast majority of people on Earth today have an undeveloped intuitive ability. Intuition can only be proactively developed through entering the inner journey. This is best done through a variety of spiritual practices rigorously pursued over a long period of time. Again it bears repeating that meditation is the fastest and most effective way of developing intuitive ability.

Meditation is an exquisitely simple process that is excruciatingly difficult to do well. Through a variety of focusing practices, like on the breath or a mantra, the goal of meditation is to gradually quiet the chattering ego mind. In that quiet that emerges, new understandings and capabilities, including expanded consciousness, gradually emerge.

When you engage in an intense, serious, and long-term meditation practice, you gradually awaken your inner knowing…your intuition. This awakening happens very slowly for most of us. Meditation is a means, not an end. It is a means to quieting the incessant chatter that goes on in our minds. One of my great teachers told me, "Meditation is what happens in the gap between your thoughts. Your job in meditation is to gradually widen those gaps." My first response when he told me this was "What gaps?" It is in the quiet…the deep, calm quiet that we begin to awaken that inner knowing powered by our intuition.

This early description reflects the conflict and contradiction between ego and God that existed early on for me. It also reflects an ongoing, evolving attempt to describe and define God.

Let me briefly describe God as I think I know Him today. The wisdom texts make it very clear that God is omnipresent…God is everywhere. God is within my physical being and everything outside of my physical being. God is omniscient. God is all-powerful and all knowing. God is in the manifested world and the un-manifest…with the latter being incomprehensible to our dualistic minds. As I said at the beginning of this chapter, God is. My soul is a spark of that divinity.

Jesus told us, "God is love." The Ageless Wisdom (detailed in a later chapter) tells us that of the seven major energy rays in the universe that the primary ray influencing our universe is the energy of love. And a more recent source, the Beatles, told us, "all you need is love." As we strengthen our connection with God through our intuition and soul we realize that a life lived with love is the richest and happiest. The core essence of who we really are is a being of love that uses love to compassionately relieve the suffering of others and to serve others unconditionally…more on this later.

God is much more than I can understand and have stated here. In later chapters, I will share additional insights into my understanding of God.

As you will see as the book progresses, my intuition communicated with me as certain provocative experiences and people came into my life. Normally these unusual and provocative experiences would have been quickly rejected by my logical mind. In these highly unusual situations, my logical mind was overwhelmingly neutralized. Outside of these unusual situations my logical mind was almost never neutralized. What ruled the day was not my logical mind but a deep inner sense that a course of action was right. I can look back now and know that it was inner knowing that trumped my logical mind. At the time and especially early on in my journey, at crucial times I felt compelled to make decisions that my logical mind did not understand or agree with. My best description is that it is a feeling of profound rightness in the decision I chose.

Encouragingly this form of communication is accessible and usually understandable to the vast majority of us. It does require the ability to look at your life through a different lens. One of the abilities is the ability to see the bigger picture of your life through the connections and interactions of multiple life events. Put another way, you connect the dots of life events. What might first seem to be a random series of events in your life will be revealed as a series of interconnected events that tell a compelling story and provide powerful and provocative insights that can enrich the balance of your life. While being older gives you more experiences to see both patterns and a big picture, I believe that even people in their 20s and 30s have enough life experience to both see patterns and bring a new perspective to events that come into their life.

All of the mystical and spiritual traditions are in clear agreement. When we incarnate into human form, we do so with a plan and set of possible learning opportunities (only a very, very few of us are aware that there is a plan and what the plan is). This plan is not defined by chance, but according to the causes we have already set in motion from previous incarnations. Much of this plan involves resolving previous life karmic obligations (and new ones we incur in the current life) but is not limited to this. (Yes, I have a deep belief and understanding of reincarnation.)

Every wisdom tradition includes karma even though it is not always called that. For example, Jesus told us "as we sow so shall we reap." This captures the heart of the meaning of karma, which is that there are consequences, good and/or bad, for every action and intention we have.

Many of life's events are rooted in karma which are the consequences of earlier choices....earlier in this life or previous lives. There is good and bad karma. When a bad karmic event occurs, it is critical to make new choices....better choices than we have in the past with a similar event. If we do not learn and use the learning to make better choices the cycle of karma will continue until we do learn....choose to learn this time. The importance of this is difficult to exaggerate...if we continue making the same negative choices in response to an event...indicating that we have not learned...then the likelihood is that the next opportunity to learn will be more intense.

Awareness that people and events in our life are learning experiences is an indirect and yet powerful way that our intuition speaks to us. It requires openness to the possibility that life is not a random and chaotic experience but there is a Divine plan.

We are given free will and judgment so that we are not "prisoners" of this plan. We can use our power to choose and act in ways that shape and define our path. We can use those powers to make progress by learning from events or repeat previous errors and even make bigger errors that require future resolution...often in another lifetime. The preferred course is to learn from events and utilize that learning to make better choices that are more in line with Universal laws and the essence of who we really are.

Ram Dass, a powerful spiritual teacher says it well, "Life is an incredible curriculum in which we live it richly and passionately as a way of awakening to the deepest truths of our being." This "curriculum" or plan is a field of learning opportunities.

In life we encounter events that provide us an opportunity to learn. If we are present and aware enough, they are an opportunity to tap into a higher-level meaning of an event. Usually this means going beyond ego and logical mind learning. Sometimes the answers can be painful to the ego, which often makes the learning difficult to accept. Increasingly as we ask these questions and our intuition grows, the learning comes through deep inner knowing that have the potential to transform our lives. Learning eventually produces growth and this growth takes all of us in the same basic direction (although often on a very zigzag course) with the same ultimate destination. I say "eventually" because for some of us the apparent learning takes us down a dark road filled with evil before making a U-turn and getting back on our path.

There are several challenges we face with "hearing" our intuition speak about the reasons and lessons behind life's events. First, when we encounter events, especially painful ones, we tend to shift our focus to others through efforts like blaming them for the pain. When we do this we lose the opportunity to garner personal learning. Second, often events prompt habitual responses. For example, every time a person yells at us we may have the same response, like walking away to avoid confrontation. When we do this, we do not fully engage the event and lose the opportunity to understand the reasons and, therefore, the learning from the event. Third, with some or even most life events we are left to wonder what it was about. Wonder and even a low level curiosity in these situations bring us closer to learning from our intuition's communication with us.

We need to go beyond wonder and curiosity to engage the messages we receive through an awakening intuition or even inklings. By engaging them we tune into a broader set of understandings. By remaining open, we can "hear" intriguing new insights and see new choices. We know they are the best for us by the feeling of lightness and rightness associated with them. Now that our intuition has communicated, what we do with the learnings is the next step in the journey. For example, most of us experience inklings in a variety of situations like while we are out running or taking a shower.

That ultimate human destination is self-realization and enlightenment that represent the highest level of human development. We arrive at this destination through a series of expansions in our consciousness, of which there are three major expansions (super, Christ, and Cosmic). This destination is part of God's plan for all of us. Avatars have shared this plan with us through several sacred wisdom texts over the last few thousand years. While the language and context varies somewhat, the meaning, direction, process, and ultimate destination do not vary. Avatars periodically come onto Earth to help us along the journey to that ultimate human destination. Jesus, Krishna, Buddha, Patanjali, and others have all come on earth to show us the way.

It also requires a broad awareness to not just see events in isolation but in context with previous or simultaneous events. Life is a big picture journey...everything....and I mean everything...is connected. The meaning of a current event can be better understood in relation to other events, sometimes in relation to broader cultural, national, and even global perspectives. This meaning can be especially helpful....and even profound...when a theme emerges between events.

As you will see in my story, a series of events built on each other. A subsequent event probably only could have happened because a previous event opened the door. Themes can reveal directions and when we see them we can then more consciously and proactively seek to move further along that theme and direction. When this happens really powerful learning....and fun...can happen.

This can be a life-changing awareness. All of a sudden people and events that seem disconnected and trigger egocentric and emotional responses can take on a much more powerful, constructive, and moving forward meaning and value. All of us, regardless of our spiritual inclination and growth can benefit from developing an awareness of this indirect way that our intuition speaks to us. Developing this awareness is sometimes almost as simple as asking questions about what people and events can teach us, especially the bigger picture teachings. These teachings can begin to emerge with even a modest diminishing of egocentric and emotional perspectives that dominate most of our lives. The learning deepens as we engage deeper forms of learning through meditation and spiritual practices.

Certainly the early part of my story is about developing this awareness that produced life-transforming insights leading to greater and greater peace, love, and joy in my life.

Let's get on with the story.

FOUR
CHAPTER

Twenty Quick Years

I was born in Salem, Massachusetts just before the end of World War II. Later in life my daughters joked about where I was born…they tell me that being born in Salem explained all of my "weirdness." Of course, they were referring to Salem's history of witchcraft.

There was nothing terribly unusual about my first twenty years on Earth. I grew up in a small New England town on the ocean. My parents, who emigrated separately from Holland and met in the United States, scraped by for most of these years. My father worked in a variety of jobs, ultimately ending up as the manager of a chain restaurant. This was a far cry from his upbringing as an officer in the Dutch merchant marine. For the most part, my mother stayed at home and raised my brother and I. As we were graduating from high school, she started a very successful local real estate business as the first Century 21 franchise in her area.

In high school I was a dedicated student who graduated in the top 5% of my very small class. I participated in some modest extracurricular activities. The most notable was Junior Achievement where I was selected as president of the year for the state of Massachusetts. I was also very deeply into the possibility of being a weatherman. I had my own complete weather station and recorded a wide range of observations and measurements twice a day for about six years. The next most notable extracurricular accomplishment was being national champion in a very small East Coast only sport, Grand Banks Dory racing. After winning the "national" championship, we did get to race against the Canadians during the three years I participated in the sport (we were trounced by the Canadians!).

Church and God were virtually absent from my life. About every four years or so my mother decided we should go to Sunday school. Immediate and often intense resistance from my brother and I terminated this initiative after a couple of weeks.

I applied to six colleges and universities and was fortunate to be accepted by all of them. I chose Penn State. When I started there, Joe Paterno was an assistant coach and by the time I left he had taken over from Rip Engle as head coach. Now that dates me!

My intention was to turn my interest in meteorology into a formal degree. A strange thing happened along the way. Before starting my Penn State classes, I took some interest and aptitude tests. These suggested that my interests were most closely aligned with someone in business or law. I still am amazed that these simple test results immediately persuaded me to change my intended major from meteorology to pre-law.

I was very active in extracurricular activities. This included being president of a major student government group on campus as well as being president of the national organization as a junior (the first person to do that). With another student, I pioneered a successful effort to bring the previously banned humor magazine, Froth, back onto campus.

I graduated with a degree in pre-law, applied to law schools, and entered law school.

FIVE
CHAPTER

Starting To Wake Up

The next twenty years were pretty uneventful except for four experiences.

Between my junior and senior year at Penn State I married a woman I had met a couple of years earlier. I met her during my college summer job as an ocean lifeguard near my hometown in Massachusetts. The early years of the marriage were on rocky ground. During my senior year of college, I had to live in the dorm as a supervisor for the Dean of Men while she lived in a small apartment. We saw each other on weekends. After my senior year of college I took two jobs that had me working seven days a week, Monday through Friday days and six days a week at a night job 30 miles from where we lived. The choices I made during this period and for some time later clearly reflected the higher priority I gave to a career and earning money over my marriage.

I entered law school with a marriage that was on the rocks. Early on in the first year, we decided to divorce which was absolutely the most painful experience of my life up until that point. I had never failed at anything (at least that's what I told myself) and I was now failing at something in spectacular fashion. I entered law school expecting a three-year draft deferment but shortly after entering the maximum deferment for graduate school was reduced to two years because of the military's need during the Vietnam Conflict.

At 6'5" tall I did not want to risk being drafted and being on the point of a patrol in Vietnam. I figured I was too big a target. I went to my local Navy recruiter and was accepted into the Officer Candidate Program where I spent the first 16 weeks of my three-year Navy career. Interestingly, my wife and I reunited at the end of this training. We spent several fairly happy years together before finally amicably ending our marriage after seven years.

After this necessary interlude in the Navy, a large consumer products company (Procter & Gamble) hired me. I began my career in sales and was promoted faster from the initial position than anyone had been before.

Fast promotions also followed in the other positions, each leading to greater responsibility. At one point, I requested to move from sales to marketing since only marketing people at P&G achieved senior leadership positions. My boss turned down my initial request, my boss's boss turned down my next request, and finally a group vice president approved my request to transfer to marketing.

This transfer meant that I went from a senior sales manager to a very junior marketing person. (Of note, I married again during this....but more on that wonderful decision later.) Again, I focused almost exclusively on my career and was again promoted very quickly through a series of positions. Before leaving, I achieved the position of marketing department head of a division, the first person from sales to achieve this in domestic operations in the previous twenty years.

After sixteen years with P&G, I moved from the central United States to the West Coast as a vice president in another consumer products company, The Gallo Winery. I spent the next ten years there, but I'm now getting ahead of myself.

Since I do not intend to discuss too much more of my business career after this brief section, I will briefly describe the kind of work I was doing to give more context to the rest of my story. The corporate environments I worked in were intense and competitive. These companies have many smart people. Standards are high. Looking back, I feel fortunate that I took a "learners" approach to all of my jobs. That meant I deeply invested energy in learning about multiple aspects of my business. My focus was on doing my best work, not on career advancement. Interestingly, by focusing on the former the latter took care of itself.

The work involved such key skills as rigorous analysis, high-level creativity, expert business writing, a logical left-brain orientation, and the ability to put all of this together to be highly persuasive, especially with senior management. Sixty-hour weeks were not unusual. I was well compensated for my work. Eventually it led to the purchase of multiple homes (sometimes for family members), luxury cars, and financial freedom.

From the very beginning of my career, I was a saver and investor. While I started off my adult life with less than $50 in my checking account, I would eventually end up with a seven-figure savings account. At one point analysis revealed that I no longer needed to work since my savings would enable me to pay my bills until I was about 100. At this point in my life I chose to leave the corporate world and embrace freedom to do what was fun and in service to others. Some of these activities will come up in later chapters since they merged to become part of the greater life journey.

Throughout this period I was a very competitive person. My ego had a very tough time losing. In tennis for example, a coach told me that he had never seen someone who was so hard on themselves. I experienced mistakes as failures. I eventually gave up tennis because I was so competitive that I was miserable.....and not very good.

Enough of the career stuff.

Now about those experiences that would shape my life......

The first of these experiences occurred in San Diego while I was in the Navy. Through some people I met at an experimental college course, I was introduced to a marijuana "mind altering" experience. This produced a remarkably different level and quality of awareness than my normal intense, competitive, and logical engagement with the world around me.

An altered mind was especially enjoyable when taken with music. This almost sounds like a recipe, which in a way it is....get high and listen to the Moody Blues. This quickly disengaged the intense, competitive, and logical awareness...replacing it was a peaceful, serene, and acute awareness of the senses. This was a remarkable and dramatic experience. Looking back,

I am a bit amazed that the experience was not frightening or disorienting. Instead, it felt very comfortable, safe, and a bit exhilarating.

An entry in my personal journal written in my cryptic journal style illustrates what I was experiencing at the time of my first "mind altering" experience.

What a night! I am amazed that it felt safe and right. A 100% positive experience. Focused on sound and words. A richness I never experienced before. Wow! A new life dimension. Has its place but a rather small one. Need to sort this out.

Music especially took on a greatly heightened role in my life, even when I was not high. I finally understood some of the Beatles later songs. Pink Floyd only seemed to make sense when I was high. Of note, this was about two-years of light experimentation that ended as quickly as it began. It seemed serve its purpose of expanding my awareness and now I wanted that awareness to be crisp, clear and fully alive.

My next experience did not involve any altered states of consciousness, but it did begin my awakening to a new way of knowing. This awakening occurred as I was attempting to make a very important decision. That decision involved who I should marry.

My first marriage occurred when I was twenty-one. In the end it was very amicable as we both recognized that we had grown up to be different people than we were when we fell in love and impulsively decided to get married.

The pain made me resolve that when I got married again I would be very analytical about the decision, unlike the impulsive decision I made before. I trusted my logical capabilities, but not my spur of the moment, emotional decisions. This led to the establishment of a checklist of attributes my next wife would have. In my first marriage I let my feelings dominate my decision-making and this time logic was going to be in charge.

During one of my assignments as a sales manager, I fell in love with Patricia who did not completely fulfill the checklist I had established. Thus, when I was promoted and moved to a different city, I decided to end the almost three year relationship.

In my new assignment, I worked at the headquarters of this large company and felt sure that I would meet a woman there who met my checklist. I began the search on the first day of my assignment. In a short period of time I was dating several women who fulfilled the checklist, but clearly held no long-term interest for me.

I maintained sporadic contact with Patricia who I'd left behind. At one point she was ready to call off the relationship in any form because it was too painful and she wanted to move on. All of a sudden I found myself faced with a real ending of the relationship.

I was strangely and deeply pained by the possibility. My logical mind said "no, do not get married" but every other aspect of my being screamed "YES"…I was not about to easily dismiss my logical mind as the ultimate decider.

I spent one agonizing weekend reflecting on the potential end of this loving relationship. The longer I agonized the more compelling the right decision became…compelling is absolutely the right word because I felt a force far bigger than my logical mind pushing me to make a marriage proposal. The more I resisted, the stronger the force became.

Another excerpt from my personal journal of the time illustrates what I was experiencing.

> *Confused! I have always trusted my logic when making important decisions. Logic says "no", but my inner sense says "yes". Wow! Even writing this I can feel my inner "yes" get even stronger. It is almost like I'm not going to be able to live with myself if I don't give in to this inner force. What is this inner force? What is it!?*

About halfway into the weekend I gave in. I dismissed my logical mind and engaged this force that led me to pick up the phone and invite her to the new city. I let go of the logical constructs that had held me prisoner. When I let go, there was an incredible sense of lightness and rightness. There was no more conflict and doubt. I was going to marry Patricia and become a father to Tricia, her daughter from a previous marriage……two very big steps for me. (I would later adopt Tricia as our daughter.)

More than thirty years later, the love is deeper than it ever was on the day of the proposal and gets deeper every single day. Dismissing my logical mind as the penultimate arbitrator was a difficult and ultimately illuminating decision. I absolutely could not explain the compelling force that overruled my logical mind, but I could not deny its existence or power. Even today as I look back on the experience, I am in awe of the compelling force that finally helped me make the right decision. (Interestingly, when Patricia read this paragraph in draft form she wrote, "It was wisdom, silly!")

While I did not recognize it at the time, looking back this appears to be the Universe (my word at the time) making it very clear that this was the path I was meant to take. At the time the only thing I was aware of was a very strong indescribable force that easily overwhelmed my logical mind, something that had never happened before in my life.

The last experience occurred when I was the sales manager for New England living in the Boston area. We met a truly remarkable couple who were about fifteen years older than we were. He had been a highly successful entrepreneur before selling the company and starting an eclectic group of new ventures in Cambridge, like a restaurant and movie theater.

Both were exceptionally intelligent having gone to schools like Princeton and Harvard Business School. The husband, Ralph, was an ardent student of the world around and in him. The latter led him to be a very serious student of Jungian psychological analysis. As a serious student, he read extensively and engaged in a personal journey of understanding with a Jungian psychologist for over a decade.

This was fascinating and entirely new for me. Prior to meeting them, I had little interest in better understanding who I was. In truth, I probably had *no* interest in better understanding who I was. All of a sudden there was a person in my life who I respected and liked on many dimensions who was really into better understanding himself. This was fascinating and heady stuff that produced many late-night conversations.

Compared to virtually no introspection prior to this experience, I began the journey of trying to better understand myself…I quickly learned this was not easy and that I had a tremendous amount to learn about myself. In addition to the late night conversations, I also began to work with his psychologist. Except for better understanding a re-occurring nightmare,

I found little value in this process except that by understanding the night-mare's meaning it never occurred again.

This relationship with this couple was unlike any other I have had in my life before this time and that I would have in the balance my life. The conversations were provocative and touched a deep inner interest I did not know was there. Here were smart and intelligent people who had been successful at the highest levels in their careers and they were inter-ested in the meaning of life and in better understanding themselves. It was intoxicating.

My personal journal was a trusted companion throughout this proc-ess. Another excerpt illustrates some of the wonder of the time.

> *Open to new possibilities. I see new possibilities. I see and care about myself and others in new ways. Exhilarating! Alive! Where does all this lead? I can't wait to see.*

Understanding myself better was a major benefit of our broader rela-tionship with them. Looking back, this was a very powerful chapter in my life where I became enchanted with the mystery of life and who I was. At the time I had little understanding of how mysterious the mystery of life really was. I thought I had unlocked important and far-reaching insights that I now see as merely small seeds that were to sprout and grow into a sort of tree of life. Just as I would have trouble imagining the first tender green sprout emerging from the earth could ever eventually become a mighty sequoia, I could not imagine at the time the doors that were about to open.

Nowhere in these experiences does the word "God" appear. That is because there was no awareness of God in my life during the first forty years or so of my life. I can only remember one conversation with a devout Mormon friend in those forty years. That conversation ended with us agreeing to disagree.

Looking back from the perspective of today, these experiences and some other smaller ones were part of my journey…a journey I was not aware existed at the time. These experiences prepared me for what was to come next. They taught me some valuable lessons. I realized that my logi-cal mind was not the only basis for making important life decisions. While at the time I could not describe what the other decision-making capability was, I could not deny its existence. Then a door opened to understanding who I was and how I could become a better person. While it seemed to be a wide-open door at the time, I later recognized it was merely a glimpse into the possible.

Life had gotten a more interesting and a lot fuller. There was a new excitement about the future and it transcended the virtually exclusive business career focus of the past.

My intuition spoke. It spoke in ways I did not see or understand at the time…but inherent in each of the events was a message, a lesson that contributed to an opening and shift in my life.

At the time I had no idea this happened. Looking back, marrying Patricia and becoming a father was one of those very sharp turns in my life, turns away from the very narrow and strict path I was on at the time. Certainly in the beginning some of the sharpest turns represented powerful times that my intuition spoke, as a part of an unfolding plan. To be clear, as the plan unfolds I maintained my will power and power of choice. It seems to me that the minor twists and turns of life can have a transitory life affect, but the larger ones are harder to ignore. Certainly that is true for this experience.

On to the next chapter……..

SIX
CHAPTER

Got My Attention

"Come on. This is such a waste!" I was clearly exasperated. I had already gotten angry. That did not work...now frustration also appeared to be failing.

I had just come home after a tough day doing battle with my boss about a project I felt strongly about. I had little energy for another battle at home....yet, here I was facing two women who were clearly excited and feeling good about what they had just agreed to. The contrast could not have been sharper between their excited, smiling faces and my frustrated frown. This event occurred as I approached my fortieth birthday and was about 14 years into my 16 year Procter & Gamble career.

The object of this frustration was Susan and my wife, Patricia. Susan was a very recent friend in the new city that we had moved to when I was promoted. Susan was a flaming New Age believer who quickly dismissed anything approaching logical thought.

Susan had an appointment the previous week with a new psychic in town. She raved about how insightful this woman was. She had done a lot of selling before I arrived on the scene. She sold Patricia on getting her own appointment with the psychic. Patricia's agreement to this plan was confounding. She had never demonstrated any interest in anything New Age or psychic......then or now.

I found myself contending with Susan's unbridled enthusiasm and Patricia's already made-up mind. It was no contest.

Before going further with the story, here's some life context at the time. I had the best job in my career at Procter & Gamble at this time. They bought a large Coca-Cola bottler headquartered in Lexington, Kentucky. I had gone down there to run it. It was an exciting time to be in the soft drink business. We introduced Diet Coke and then New Coke that was both controversial and fun. We went to the Kentucky Derby. I had great seats at the final four college basketball championship when it was held in town. We had dinner at the governor's mansion. Interestingly, it was during this period that Patricia and I had the blessing of a semi-miracle baby.....our youngest of two daughters. It was a wondrous time and I could barely imagine where it would lead to in the future. Back to the story....

Having lost the battle, I figured I could still win the war. In frustration I said that I would accompany Patricia on her appointment. My expressed purpose was to expose the psychic as a fraud. There was no way, I thought, that any stranger could know the answers to the kinds of questions I was going to ask. I was supremely confident about my ultimate success.

The figurative piece of two by four wood to my head mentioned in an earlier chapter was now poised over my head. I was about to receive a thumping that would leave a lasting impression. I was about to wake up, never knowing that I had been asleep.

The Saturday 10 AM appointment was upon us. After a fainthearted last-minute attempt to not go failed, we drove the two minutes to her house. Her house was about half mile from our house. As we arrived, there did not seem to be anything special about this tract home.

After a pleasant greeting, Denise ushered us into a small kitchen table that we all sat around. She told us a little bit about herself. She had recently moved from New York City to marry her new husband. In New York City she was frequently quoted as a psychic in the tabloid newspapers. She now found herself in a medium sized southern city that knew nothing about her. She explained that we could ask any questions during our one-hour appointment and that the entire session would be recorded.

The session began with Patricia asking some questions about the meaning of some recent events in our life. Denise's answers sounded right, but not especially insightful. This went on for about ten minutes and the consistency of Denise's right sounding answers were starting to make an impression on me.

We got to a point where the answers started referring to things in our past. It was at this point that I started asking questions. I asked for the name of Patricia's first husband. Without hesitation, Denise gave the right answer. I then asked where he lived, and again Denise was right without any hesitation. I asked for the name of his current wife, and again she was right. No one in the city that we lived in...other than Patricia and I... could possibly have known this information.

I then moved to ask a series of questions about my past. What town did I grow up in? (It was an obscure small town in a state hundreds of miles away.) What was the name of my first wife? (A common first name and an unusual last name) Where did she live when I met her? (A small town in another state) How long have we been married? In what city did we get divorced? (A large city in California, but no mention of California had been made in any context before this question.) Where were my parents born? (In another country) What was my brother's name? (A rather uncommon first name) Where did he live? (In a state that had not been mentioned yet)

I was absolutely stunned. Her quick responses were 100% correct. Again, even Patricia did not know all the answers to all these questions and certainly no one in the city that we were living at the time knew any of these answers.

How could Denise know the answer to these questions? I looked at Patricia, our eyes met, and she could see that I was more than perplexed by this situation.

Patricia then reentered the conversation. She asked several questions about the future. At the time there was obviously there was no way of calibrating the correctness of Denise's answers and they sounded a little far-fetched. Having said that, I could not dismiss her answers given her extreme accuracy about events and places in my past. (Looking back at the future predictions they were as inaccurate as her understanding of our past was accurate.)

At the end of the hour we thanked her and collected our tape recording of the session. Disbelieving my own ears, I immediately listened to the tape when we returned home. My ears had not deceived me. I had heard what I had heard. That did not make any of this any easier.

Understanding the context in which this event occurred is important to understanding my reaction. I was a very logical person with a strong left-brain orientation. I thought that I knew almost everything and what I didn't know was of little value to me. I had a very high level of confidence in my ability to understand events. While my logical thinking had been trumped in the decision to marry Patricia, I had quickly dismissed the "force" that seemed to compel this decision. I couldn't understand this "force" and it seemed to be an anomaly of some sort. Since I could not understand it, I did not let it in any way undermine my confidence in the power of my logical mind.

The experience with Denise changed all that. The experience was undeniable. She had a method of knowing information that my logical mind could never understand. Denise had not used logic to answer the questions. The best I could figure out at the time was that she had access to some unknown source. I had already quickly ruled out fraud.

My personal journal reveals very simply what I was feeling at the time.

What just happened??!! I don't know.

If I were to take the time to conduct a search of all of my journal writings prior to this moment, I am sure I would not find the sentence "I don't know" since I thought I always had the answer.

For several hours I was stunned. Never in my life have I been so clueless about something so undeniably true. Rather quickly my logical mind and ego started damage control. They again took center stage in my consciousness with the apparent purpose of minimizing damage to my self-perception, ego, and confidence.

The damage control was effective against these objectives, but it could not completely obscure this powerful life event. I briefly endured the "told you so" from Susan and then appeared to move on with my life. I moved on because there was no apparent path to greater understanding. For the near term it would remain a conundrum.

But the seed had been planted. As I now look at the events that unfolded over the next several years, I realize that the experience with Denise was the "headwater" of a journey that would ebb and flow over decades.

Years later when I was further along in my journey I gained some additional perspective on this event. My guru (who you'll meet in a later chapter) said, "Pride is blinding." Clearly, this applied to me at the time my experience with Denise. He went on to add, "Humbleness is the open gate through which the divine flood of Mercy and Power loves to flow into receptive souls." At this time in my life I only knew how to spell "humble" and "humility" but as life progressed I fortunately became increasingly familiar with these very useful self-balancers.

I fought to avoid this event. I conspired to reveal the event as a fraud. I failed at both efforts. This was even a bigger sharp turn in my life than the one in the previous chapter. There was an initial thrust in my life to challenge my fundamental beliefs and understandings about how the world worked. It clearly was a part of the unfolding plan. While my ego's inclination was to ignore what had just happened and even deny that it had happened, the truth lie in the recording. There was no denying it happened.

At that time I had no sense that my intuition had spoken. In fact, I never thought about my intuition or God.

Interestingly, the events of the previous chapter and this chapter combined mightily to create the inner conditions that made future steps of opening to my intuition possible. As big as these openings were at the time, they would be just the beginning, but of course I had no awareness of this at the time.

I had no conscious awareness of the lessons I had learned from the events of the last two chapters at the time they happened. Looking back when awareness did start to develop, I could see how I learned subtle, yet very powerful lessons. These lessons opened doors I could never imagine at the time. From the perspective of today, this experience made all the wonderful events that were to unfold possible. From the same perspective, I am still amazed how this event could even enter into my life given my extreme left brain, know it all life orientation I had at the time. Clearly, something unusual and highly powerful happened. If looked at as an isolated event, it can seem insignificant. When put into the context of what was about to come, it was profound.

SEVEN
CHAPTER

The Book

Shirley MacLaine emerged into my awareness about a year later. She had written books and been interviewed about communicating with the dead via psychics. If the experience with Denise had never occurred, I would not have spent one nanosecond of my awareness on such a story.

But Denise had happened and I was aware and still confused. Denise got my attention and my attention now focused on Shirley MacLaine's work. I had very little knowledge of who she was but I quickly learned that she was a skilled and highly respected actress.

I read her most popular book at the time, *Dancing in the Light*, and was intrigued. Here was a highly respected person having experiences that had many similarities to the one I had with Denise. Both were getting accurate and insightful information from an apparently non-earthly source. This popular and provocative 1986 book was quickly followed by her 1987 movie *Out on a Limb*. In a very short period of time, she brought a fringe topic into the mainstream of conversation by hundreds of thousands of people.

While engaging her works broadened my small base of understanding of psychics, it did nothing to deepen my understanding of what the heck was going on. It was clear to me now that something very real was happening....and that understanding alone sustained an intensifying curiosity.

At the time of this event, we had moved away from Lexington and were back in Cincinnati. The job I had with Procter & Gamble at the time was one of my least liked and was my last job there before leaving.

In the midst of all of this Shirley MacLaine stuff, I again had one of those perplexing experiences where a decision was made via a clearly non-logical process.

It started when I decided to learn more about what she was describing. I wasn't sure what "more" meant, so I headed off to the only New Age bookstore within a couple hundred miles...even though reading a book was something I seldom did at the time.

The New Age bookstore was in a somewhat hard to find location near the university. Parking was limited but I felt lucky when I found a space within a block of the store. The store was in an older building in need of sprucing up. As I entered, I did not know what to expect. When I walked in, I did not immediately see anything that caught my eye. For some reason I found myself walking to the back right-hand corner of the bookstore. It was almost like I knew what I wanted and where it was...when the truth was I had no idea what I wanted and where to start my search based on anything logical.

When I reached the back right corner of the bookstore, on the second shelf from the top and on the right-hand side of that shelf I found myself immediately reaching for a book. The book's title was *Living with Joy, Keys to Personal Power and Spiritual Transformation*. While I only looked at the cover page, I did not put the book back on the shelf as I continued to look at others in the area. Even when I moved my search to other parts of the bookstore, this book remained firmly in my grasp. After about twenty minutes of exploring I still had only this book in my hand as I headed for the checkout counter.

Since it was early Saturday morning when I bought the book, I had the rest of the weekend to begin reading it. As I read it, I was overwhelmed with a sense of lightness and joy that I had seldom felt in my life and never felt before when I read a book. At the time it felt like a life-changing event. Those moments don't happen very often.

The following is a sampling of chapter titles and sections that I highlighted.

- Chapter title: You Can Live Joyfully.
- "You will have joy only when you focus on having it and settle for nothing less."
- "If you wish to be aware of the higher good happening in your own life, be willing to let go of a limited perspective and enlarge the view of your life."
- "Everything that happens is meant to help move you into your greater self."
- "Every time you say a negative word to yourself or make yourself wrong, your emotional body changes its vibration and your energy drops.... Once you take responsibility and attune your awareness to higher thoughts, creating joyful images in your mind, you can raise the vibration of your emotional body."
- "Trust yourself and believe you can create what you want."
- Chapter title: Life Need Not Be Hard.
- Chapter title: Higher Purpose Is Always Something You Love.

Since 1986 when this book was published, these thoughts have become more pervasive in both the New Age and broader culture. But in the late 1980s and certainly in the central part of the United States where I lived at the time, this was a very new way of thinking.

While I did not know it when I bought the book, I quickly discovered that this was a "channeled" (for many people this is another word for psychic) book by the author, Sanaya Roman. The source was Orin, a self-described "Master Life." This sounded very much like the experiences described by Shirley MacLaine. The first chapter describes the author's first encounter with Orin via an Ouija board and gradually building her capacity to "tune into" Orin's transmissions. If I had not had the experiences with Denise and Shirley's work, I would have quickly dismissed all of this as a waste of time.

Importantly, the book's credibility was only secondarily based on its source. The primary source of credibility was the joy I felt inside as I read its messages. It was nothing short of an amazing experience. Here was an intense, left brained, and Type A person finding instant credibility in something that had no logical foundation. Its only foundation was the inner sense of truth and joy I experienced as I read the book.

I was so inspired by what I read that I immediately started recording major sections of the book onto cassettes. I had an old, clunky tape player that I was surprised to discover could also record. After learning about the right buttons to push, I began the process of recording. Gradually I developed a rhythm and my misspoken words declined.

I had about a forty-minute ride to work each morning and I played the cassettes on both my trip to and from work. The ride was mostly on an interstate so I could get in the middle lane on the drive to and from work and focus fairly well on the tape. I did this every day for months. Prior to this experience, I had never listened to anything other than occasional music on a cassette…and I had never spent hours recording a book onto a tape so I could listen to it at any time.

My clear purpose for listening to this every day for more than an hour was to bring about personal transformation. I was not living in accordance with the inspired messages in the book, and deeply and intensely wanted a life that was guided by the book's insights. I realized the only way I was going to have a chance to bring about such tremendous change was to commit myself to an intense and focused effort to "get" the book's insights and messages.

In addition, at the end of each chapter was a series of questions in a planning section on how to implement the insights from the chapter. I completed 100% of these sections. I had never done these activities with any book I have ever read before.

My personal journal wonderfully captured what I was feeling during this time.

I feel new. There are new possibilities I'd never imagined would be possible in my life. These are exhilarating possibilities filled with hope. I don't think I have ever been so inspired, so motivated to achieve something so desirable.

Over the years I reread the book more than ten times. Again, this was a first for me. Each time I reread it, I realized new and deeper insights. When the period between readings was six months or more, it almost felt like I was reading it for the first time.

From the perspective of today, I clearly see how the Denise and Shirley MacLaine experiences prepared me for this book. In fact, without the Denise experience, Shirley would have been dismissed as a "Hollywood kook." Today there is also the understanding that the energy softening experiences that preceded Denise and Shirley also paved the way by getting me in touch with something other than a dominant left-brain orientation. I cannot help but be impressed by this apparent "plan" to begin my awakening.

From the same perspective, my intuition played virtually no role in my thinking and awareness *at the time*. There was only passing consideration that Denise's source might be my intuition, but that was quickly dismissed. I dismissed it then because I had so little understanding of what my intuition was, but I certainly didn't think that my intuition communicated so directly with humans.

Today, I cannot help but be impressed that this was an unknowing experience of my intuition speaking to me. My logical mind was disengaged and I related to an experience from an entirely new basis for knowing, at least new to me. While the book did not dwell on my intuition, my intuition and God were clearly part of the book's message. Having previously avoided books that talked about my intuition or God, I found a surprising comfort and rightness with the mention of my intuition in the context of this book.

Several years later I looked back and I clearly realized these feelings as strong inner knowing…intuitive knowing…guidance from my soul…. guidance from the Divine.

I feel like I was nothing less than "guided" from the front of the bookstore to the back right-hand corner to find the book *Living With Joy*. There is certainly a deep sense that this was "meant to be." When I read the book, my logical mind remained disengaged. There was no skepticism or judging going on. There was complete openness. I warmly embraced the book's insights because they felt so right. I took concrete actions (recording cassettes and developing written plans) because something "felt so right." The process of finding it and the impact it had on me exceeded any single book I had read before this time.

In the context of the time, this was a startling change. I almost never did anything just because it felt right. I did things because logic and judgment dictated it was the right thing to do.

While I could not appreciate it at the time, my life journey had come to a fork in the road. With *Living With Joy* as my initial guidebook, I chose "the road less traveled." (Scott Peck so richly brought this language to life in his book with the same title.) My spiritual awakening went from an occasional event that lasted for a couple of days at most to a major item on my daily "to do" list....a list that was a considerable daily guiding force.

My intuition or my wisdom mind spoke. At the end of this third major sharp turn in my life, I began thinking about my intuition and God for the first time and about a possible unfolding plan for my life. To be clear, it was the beginning...it was an inkling.

Awareness of a bigger picture and plan were emerging. I was beginning to look for the meaning of an event and, very importantly, how it could shape future events. In some cases I would seek out events and others happened unexpectedly. As you will see, even some events I sought out had far more profound impacts than I ever imagined going into them.

For the first time I was open to greater meaning leading to greater possibilities. The sense of excitement and curiosity were steadily increasing....my journey and exploration into the unknown was proving to be the best part of my life.

It changed my life. I looked at life more positively. I felt glimmers of joy about life's possibilities. I could feel that I was in the process of changing both my values and compass I use to navigate life. While my earlier experience with my friend Ralph opened the door crack into self-awareness and self-improvement, the door now swung wide open. With various degrees of consistency, I engaged a life of personal growth. Again, prior to this the only growth I was interested in was career and financial growth. In the context of the times, this was profound change I knew at some level would last the rest of my life.

Looking back, it is clear that this is when I began to live a wisdom inspired life. I had a strong intuitive connection with this book. I was reading was deep truths from the clearest wisdom source I had encountered up to this time. It inspired me to begin a fundamental transformation of who I was.

It's just what I would expect if my intuition spoke.

EIGHT
CHAPTER

Psychics Get Personal....Again

For almost the next ten years, my life theme was about "exploration and growth."

The exploration started while I still lived in Cincinnati in the last years of my Procter & Gamble career. I took a brief course on past lives (independently offered and not associated with any educational institution) over a few weekends.

During one of the classes, the instructor led an exercise that was a combination guided meditation and past life regression. At the time, I had briefly explored topics like reincarnation and past life regressions, but only enough to have a small sense of possibilities. Meditation, guided or not, was not a part of my life and I knew very little about it. I had no special connection with the instructor other than he had modest credibility because he felt he knew enough to attract about seven people to his course.

In this exercise, we were asked to close our eyes and become "quiet," whatever that meant. Again, looking back I was surprised that I could so completely suspend my judging mind because during the week in my job it was constantly on high.

I experienced a quick but very rich awakening to a period in the 1700s or 1800s....it was like an instant dream state except that I had not gone to sleep. In vivid detail I saw a cobblestone street lined with shops. I found myself walking slightly downhill on this cobblestone street towards a harbor. When I looked down I not only saw the cobblestone street but I also saw my feet and I seemed to be appropriately dressed for the historical time period. In the harbor I saw fairly large sailing vessels representative of the kind you see in that historical time. The entire experience felt like it was only a minute or less....but it could have been longer because I lost track of time. As quickly as the experience started, it ended.

As vivid and as real as the experience felt, I did not know what to make of it. While it had occurred in the context of a guided meditation and was intended to connect us with a previous life, it did not feel like it was part of a previous life or that it was not a part of a previous life...it just was. What it was is still a mystery to me today.

My exploration intensified when I left Procter & Gamble in the late 1980s. We moved to Northern California and I took a job as a vice president of marketing at the Gallo Winery. The highlight of this job in the early years was developing Bartles and Jaymes advertising with Frank and Ed. This was a highly successful advertising campaign that was purposely humorous. It was the only time in my career in a meeting with senior management that we knew we had success when people laughed at proposed new advertising for the brand.

One of my first steps was to better understand the channeling phenomenon. After reviewing Bay Area newspapers and information sources, I identified four people who claimed to channel and told a pretty good story in their ads. I set up four Saturday appointments.

Overall, the experience was discouraging. Three of the four had no credibility since they could not correctly identify any details from my past and their overall process seemed to be more fantasy than fact.

Fortunately, one of the four was a gold mine psychic and channeling connection. José is a fascinating person. He holds a Ph.D. in psychology, is a Navajo trained shaman, and a very clear channel for Michael. Several people claim they can channel Michael. Michael, it seems, is a group soul, a collective consciousness of 1,050 essences who finished all their lifetimes on earth, cycled off the physical plan and now teach from the mid-causal plane (casual is our third of three bodies, physical, astral and then casual). While I found all of this interesting, as a starting point it had little or no credibility for me. At the time, I had no understanding of the "casual world," any form of "life after death," and reincarnation was still a work in progress for me.

José wrote several books on the world according to Michael. More precisely, they are primarily focused on what can be best called "spiritual psychology." My first conversations with José/Michael centered on a description of my personality that resonated very positively and accurately with me. It was an expansive, in-depth conversation that felt completely true to me. Some discussions of specific events in my past confirmed that José had Denise-like capabilities also. When I shifted the conversational focus from myself to other family members (who José had never met), his personality descriptions were universally precise and accurate.

Listening to Jose/Michael I heard my personality described in terms that were familiar and credible. I also heard some new insights, like the fact that, according to José/Michael, I was an old soul. At the time I had little understanding of what this meant, but later came to understand that I had experienced many, many incarnations. Another insight that emerged was that my life purpose was aligned around various ways of serving others. I will revisit this insight in a later chapter.

Following my first session with José, I read a number of his books, which deepened my connection and belief in his abilities. Over the next ten years I had about ten sessions with him. All of the sessions provided helpful insights and deepened his credibility with me, with one very notable exception. 100% of José/Michael's predictions of the future ranged from highly inaccurate to nothing remotely like the suggested future possibilities ever manifested. When José/Michael looked at my world from the perspective of the past or present, the insights and observations were universally true either based on logic or a deep inner sense of truth. I did not have an understanding (and still do not today) about why both Denise and his predictions of the future were so inaccurate.

Two of the sessions involved other family members and the results were extraordinary. The first of these two involved my youngest grandson. At a very young age he experienced serious, intense psychological and physiological problems. Work with traditional medical resources provided a somewhat mixed analysis, although one diagnosis seemed to continually emerge. Less than 1% of young children his age have this diagnosis.

Since the problem was serious and solutions more ambiguous than either his parents or I were comfortable with, I decided to seek José/Michael's perspective. At the time José lived in a city a couple hundred miles from where I lived and several hundred miles from where my grandson lived. As a result, we conducted a telephone session and I sent him a picture of my grandson looking directly into the camera.

Prior to this I had never discussed my grandson with José/Michael. When the session started I asked a very open-ended question, "As you look at my grandson, what do you see?" After a brief pause, José/Michael gave me the predominant medical diagnosis. His diagnosis showed no physical clues on his body. Remember, I gave no indication that there was anything wrong with my grandson. In response to my question he could have talked about his personality, the kinds of activities he likes, and many other possibilities. Instead the first thing he provided was a medical diagnosis that 99% of children his age do not have. I was impressed and stunned at the same time.

The session continued with many helpful insights. First, there were some thoughts on the proper medical treatment and the urgency of getting his medical condition under control. Second, there were very helpful insights into the role this condition was playing in his current life, especially the karmic connection with his mother (my oldest daughter). Third, there were very helpful insights for his mother and how she could psychologically maintain the compassionate and helpful assistance she was providing. His parents found this feedback exceptionally helpful.

My personal journal captured some of the raw emotion I experienced.

Stunned.... Again! I had tears in my eyes and gratitude in my heart for the wonderful insights into a terribly important issue for (my grandson). There is now a wonderful sense of hope about the future. Without question lots of hard work remains to be done. But we now have a comprehensive medical plan and life understanding to guide the work that needs to be done.

The second of these two notable sessions involved my youngest daughter who was a teenager at the time. She also faced a serious, intense physiological and psychological problem. To help her with this we sought out the best medical and psychological resources we could find. Despite trying multiple resources, minimal progress was being made. Again, I felt it would be helpful to seek José/Michael's perspective.

I sent José a picture of my daughter looking into the camera and my daughter joined me on the telephone session. The first question that I asked José/Michael was, "As you look at my daughter, what do you see?" This very open-ended question could lead to a wide range of potential responses. Instead, he immediately gave the correct medical and psychological diagnosis. My daughter, who had had no prior experience with anything like José/Michael, was stunned. Both of us then asked a series of follow-up questions that ultimately revealed the powerful psychological forces in play here. Despite work with two psychiatrists prior to this, she had gained virtually no valuable insights from this extensive work. Now she found herself talking to a stranger who immediately provided her with insights that proved personally true. She later took this tape-recorded conversation and played it many times to help her deepen her understanding and to recover. She was ultimately successful in this effort and has repeatedly pointed to the session as the turning point.

My personal journal reflects some of the impact this had on my life at the time.

I will never forget the look on her face. Tears were mixed with a smile. She was hearing for the first time her truth which opened the door out of the prison she felt she was in. It was her first experience with this unexpected source that helped to set her free. I'm guessing it will not be her last.

Finding and working with José/Michael concluded my exploration of the channeling and psychic worlds. I knew what I wanted to know. It was helpful but not my primary resource or path in life. That would become clearer a little bit later.

What had become clear at this stage was startling to me. In about five years from the first Denise experience to Shirley MacLaine to José/Michael I had done a lot of waking up on one dimension. I started out thinking that psychic or channeling experiences were impossible and fraudulent. Five years later I found myself deeply believing and appreciating it is a valuable source of help along my journey. I was able to understand myself better and help others in powerful ways. Importantly, no alternative source could provide the quality of insights.

I also learned that not all psychics/channelers are the same. They are a medium for communication from the astral world. Their ability to be calm and centered while turning off their judgmental minds determines whether they are a clear channel or one that has only fragments of truth. Since there is no independent certification, I needed to work with many before finding a couple that were especially helpful.

For me today this is an occasional resource. Its more important ongoing role for me is a compelling confirmation that there is a powerful unseen world beyond his waking consciousness reality. For a person who entered this journey with a very strong left-brain orientation, this serves as a powerful bridging experience to some broader spiritual foundations. For this I am deeply grateful.

By this time in my life I started to regularly meditate for the first time. The process of meditation is exquisitely simple and excruciatingly difficult to do. The "exquisitely simple" part is that you sit with a straight back, usually with eyes closed, and then focus on your breathing or a mantra (often as simple as a sacred word which for me was the word love). The purpose is to let your mind settle. Again easily said but "excruciatingly difficult" to accomplish with any level of proficiency and consistency.

When I first tried meditating, I became all too familiar with the chattering mind. Seemingly random jumps from one subject to another dominated my awareness. Even many, many years later I am still challenged by the ever-chattering mind. At this time in my life, I meditated about 15 minutes early in the morning. To accommodate this in my life I started getting up around 5:30 AM instead of my normal 6 AM.

My soul spoke through my intuition during these events.

By this time I knew that psychics were not channeling God. While they were not the voice of God, the high level of spiritual development of the psychics' sources enabled them to reveal highly credible insights. While many of the insights were personal, many also addressed the bigger picture of the world around me and the laws that governed it.

My intuition spoke indirectly through revealing more details of my plan that included connections to people who could assist in my awakening. These people provided insights into who I was that felt right... insights that started to reveal the outline of a deeper picture of me and the previously "hidden" spiritual world. My awakening was happening at a pace that was comfortable....which sounds a bit strange since it was in such sharp contrast to the business part of my life.

The inputs from psychics were a very interesting and helpful mix of personal perspective to create credibility and a sort of Spirituality 101. Looking back I can easily see how this was preparing me for higher-level "courses" that would come later. Beyond question this was a logical next step in the unfolding sequence of steps along my journey.

By this time I trusted my inner knowing more and connecting with Jose/Michael felt very right...despite the sharp contrast with my work life where inner knowing was subservient to left brain processing. The events with my grandson and youngest daughter had a profound impact because the insights went beyond interesting stuff to life saving stuff... certainly in the case of my daughter. These lessons provided dramatic proof that lifted my understanding and belief to a high level that would prepare to embrace even bigger sources and connections.

At this time I was starting to clearly see connections between this and previous events....there was a theme and direction. From the perspective at the time, expanding my awareness of and experience with channeling/ psychics made sense. I had some intriguing and positive experiences prior to venturing on this expanded exploratory. From the perspective of today, I see an additional meaning. These experiences were very personal. Especially the work with José/Michael expanded my reality paradigm to include spiritual principles that built on *Living with Joy*. The world was starting to make more sense and the behaviors I wanted to manifest in this world became even clearer.

With these new experiences and connections, my wisdom inspired life moved into a higher gear. The wisdom I was tapping into had great consistency between the sources both in terms of substance and tone.

While I could not guess at the time what would later emerge, there was a strong sense of excitement about what the future held. The lessons and messages were increasingly shifting the balance of power in my life from a strong career focus to a strong spiritual focus…especially its many dimensions, as I would discover over the next several chapters.

NINE
CHAPTER

The Quantum World

The psychic and channeling experiences were not the only events to challenge my strong left brain orientation that produced my reality paradigm. I next experienced a frontal attack on my reality paradigm from the ultimate left brain source, science. The "attack" seemed to expand when I started to repeatedly encounter scientific understandings that seriously undermined my existing worldview. Now that left brain science challenged my world view.....I did not stand a chance.

Interestingly it started with a growing fascination with quantum physics. During this exploration phase I first encountered the quantum world in a very popular book titled *The Dancing Wu Li Masters* by Gary Zukav. It was the first popular book that made the quantum world reasonably accessible to a much broader audience. He followed up with *Seat of the Soul*, which led him to become a recurring guest on Oprah's show.

Prior to this fascination, I had almost no interest in science. I had not read a science book since college. I barely paid attention to news stories on science. My initial interest in quantum physics was entirely driven by the spirituality that emerged into my life starting with *Living with Joy*.

It seems strange to say it but my newfound interest in science was initiated by my newfound interest in spirituality. While my focus in this chapter is on quantum physics, I also explored what is called "new biology" which is a mixture of physics and biology, as best I can understand. There was also a later considerable exploratory into medical science, primarily through the writings of Deepak Chopra and a little bit of Norman Cousins and a few others.

Through my years of study of the quantum world with the aid of quantum physicists who can communicate in terms that non-quantum physicists can understand, I have come to view quantum physics as the first strong meeting point between spirituality and science. The quantum world is an extraordinarily different world than the Newtonian world. The quantum world is all about energy and its vast interconnectedness. The quantum world is not a chaotic and random. David Bohm, the great English quantum physicist who Einstein deeply respected, noted that the quantum world appeared to have a "guiding hand." The quantum world recognizes a great intelligence and precision that is awesome to behold.

The following series of events in my life represent both a fascinating and unsettling phase of my life that ultimately came together as a powerful integration of science and wisdom-based spirituality. At a deep level, I realized there was nothing random about how I was presented with the opportunities to learn more about science, especially the conundrums of science. For a long time I had a light interest in science, the events that unfolded in this phase of my life provided both a bridge and permission for my left brain to start relinquishing its dominating role as the definer of my worldview.

It may sound strange that left brain thinking and the quantum view of the world might be different....because isn't science left brain? Yes.... but the quantum world view is mind snapping because so much left brain thinking depends on inputs from our five senses. In the quantum world our five senses are not very helpful....at least not for me.

Understanding the quantum world of pure energy started to emerge through reading about some rather simple yet powerful scientific tests. For example, for over 100 years many scientists conducted tests to determine if one person can read the thoughts of another person. The standard methodology for this testing is to assemble cards where each card has one of five different symbols, like a circle, square, triangle, et cetera. A deck of 25 cards is completed with five cards of each symbol that are then shuffled.

One person turns over a card and then attempts to transmit the image to another person. In these tests the other person could be in another room in the same building, in another building, in a lead shielded room, or on another continent. The second person writes down the "message" or "image" they received. Scientists then tabulate the results attempting to determine the correct guess rate.

Scientists at the Stanford Research Institute in 1985 conducted a meta-analysis by combining the results from 2,549 studies completed over a thirty years by numerous researchers in many different countries. If the receiver in the studies was *not* accurately perceiving any of the messages sent to them, researchers would of expected a 20% correct guess (based on having a one in five chance of success), much as you would expect a 50% correct guess in a coin flip situation.

Instead researchers in this meta-analysis found over a 33% correct guess rate by people with no prior experience or training in this. Clearly the receivers in these studies were successful well beyond random chance. In fact, the odds against chance being the explanation for the high success rate were a million billion to one.

When I first read these results, I wasn't quite sure what I was reading. Then it hit me. To some significant degree a person can read or receive the thoughts of another person. Science now knew this beyond a shadow of a doubt. How does that happen? Science was and is clueless.

Additional meta-analytical studies drew similar conclusions. First, scientists at the Stanford Research Institute conducted a meta-analysis of clairvoyant research. In this research one individual is attempting to read a card that has been turned over at a remote location. In clairvoyant research, there is only a reader, not a sender and receiver. Again, the research concluded that the correct read rate was much higher than random chance and that the odds against chance being the explanation of the outcome were a billion billion to one.

Princeton University researchers conducted a meta-analysis of whether individuals could influence the number that came up in the throwing of a die. Again, the research concluded that the thrower of the die was able to influence the outcome at a far greater rate than chance would suggest so that the odds against chance being the explanation of the outcome were a billion to one.

Stepping back from these three major meta-analytical studies conducted by top research organizations, the conclusion is that humans have abilities to read another person's thoughts, to "see" a remote event, and use the power of their thinking to influence a physical outcome. What makes these results even more impressive is that the subjects in the research had no prior training or proven abilities. While fascinating in their own right, these results are suggestive of something far more important.

First, science understands "what" is occurring but is virtually clueless about "how" or "why" these results could occur. Quantum physics comes closest to understanding that everything in our world is interconnected energy.

Second, for about the last 500 years science has been the "ultimate definer of reality." Science started its ascension to this throne first with the publication of a paper by Copernicus concluding that the sun was at the center of our universe, not the earth. Galileo later built on this work and published his own similar conclusions. For this he paid a heavy price. He was forced to recant by the church (if he did not he would have been excommunicated) and imprisoned in various ways for the rest of his life. What is most noteworthy is that the existing "ultimate definer of reality" at the time was the church. Instead of using scripture to understand reality, Copernicus and Galileo (and many others after them) used scientific observation and mathematical calculations to understand reality. The inadequacy of the church's explanation of the relationship of the sun and the earth was the beginning of the emergence of science as the new "ultimate definer of reality."

Today we are faced with similar situation where science cannot explain unquestionable facts. As in the time of Copernicus and Galileo, when the existing paradigm (then the church and science today) cannot explain known phenomena then the conditions exist for the emergence of a new paradigm or "ultimate definer of reality."

Third, the new and emerging "ultimate definer of reality" is wisdom since the wisdom traditions can explain the "how" and "why" that science does not understand. I will address this more in a later chapter.

Quantum physics has also revealed other insights that clearly show the world is not as it appears and as we have come to think of it. Most startling and mind snapping of these conclusions is that there is no solid matter in our universe. Everything is energy. In fact, everything is an electromagnetic wave of energy.

As scientists' powerful microscopes went from molecules to atoms to protons and electrons to quarks and deeper they finally discovered that there was a vast space between whirling packets of energy. There is nothing solid about matter. Nothing.

At first I thought this was speculative thought by the quantum physicists I was reading at the time. Nothing could be further from the truth. As best I can determine, it is unanimous among quantum physicists that all of reality, all that we consider to be solid matter, is nothing more than an electromagnetic wave of energy. Of course, because of the rate of vibration it appears to be solid to our eyes and touch. Also because of electromagnetic laws, one apparently solid entity may not be able to penetrate another because of the relationship between the electromagnetic force fields.

Here are several quotes from scientists who understand that everything is energy, not solids.

- Dr. Fritjof Capra: "Quantum theory demolished the classical concept of solid objects."
- Dr. Even Walker: "Matter actually is tiny specks in a vast void."
- Dr. Deno Kazanis, biophysicist, in *The Reintegration of Science and Spirituality.*
  - "Thanks to quantum mechanics, we know that matter isn't solid. Atoms aren't solid things."
  - "Our ability to see, touch, taste, smell, and hear the world is really only due to atoms' electric charge."
  - "The reason we can hold an apple in our hand and it doesn't fall through is because the apple in our hand is made of charged atoms and our hand is made of charged atoms, so they can't interpenetrate."

What makes this understanding so difficult is that we traditionally rely on our five senses to define reality. Understanding that there is nothing solid and that all matter is an electromagnetic wave is well beyond the capability of most people to understand since they rely so extensively on their five senses. This is a mind snapping scientific truth.

The ultimate value of the science part of this life exploratory was that it brought me closer to wisdom-based spirituality. As I will discuss later, on a parallel path during this time I became a serious student of wisdom-based spirituality. The wisdom-based spiritual systems have understood the quantum insights for centuries and provide a context for understanding.

A brief entry in my personal journal reflects some of what I was feeling at the time.

> *I knew/hoped that science would somehow, sometime start to "discover" spiritual truths. There is comfort in what I've been reading lately, but for the first time there is a sense that Western science has critical limitations when it comes to understanding the bigger world in which we live.*

What helped me to see that science, especially quantum physics, and wisdom-based spirituality were increasingly in agreement were the insights of the greatest scientist in the last 100 years. Albert Einstein, who Time magazine selected as their "man of the century" in the year 2000, saw this connection. In my opinion, he was not only our greatest scientist but also a great mystic. The following Einstein quotes help to illustrate this.

- "The most beautiful emotion we can experience is the mystical. It is the power of all true art and science. He to whom this emotion is a stranger, who can no longer wonder and stand rapt in awe, is as good as dead."
- "To know that what is impenetrable to us really exists, manifesting itself as the highest wisdom and the most radiant beauty, which our dull faculties can comprehend only in their most primitive forms—this knowledge, this feeling, is at the center of true religiousness. In this sense, and in this sense only, I belong to the rank of devoutly religious men."
- "Reality is merely an illusion, albeit a very persistent one."
- "Not everything that can be counted counts, and not everything that counts can be counted."

- "My religion consists of a humble admiration of the illimitable superior spirit who reveals himself in the slight details we are able to perceive with our frail and feeble minds."

As I studied wisdom-based spirituality I increasingly recognized that it had the answers to science's conundrums. Today, I am not as intensely into the role of science, but do remain alert for occasional new developments. One other dimension of science (discussed in the next chapter) played an important role in helping my left-brain worldview transition to a wisdom-based spirituality worldview.

My feelings during this exploratory phase were mostly ones of exhilaration. First, there was a fascination with so much provocative learning. Second, both the science and wisdom-based spirituality study were seeing the same, not different, world. After decades of believing that spirituality and science had irreconcilable differences, their reconciliation profoundly influenced what became a rather rapid change in fundamental beliefs and how I lived my life. What an exciting experience!

In many ways this was one of the more subtle experiences. My awareness of the quantum world came in through unexpected sources that frankly I could easily have ignored but did not. There was something inside of me (my intuition) that said, "Pay attention." Again, I was rewarded for listening. During this time in my life I was becoming increasingly respectful of people and information that came into my life. Instead of rejecting it, I decided to "dance" with it to see if there was some value.

My quantum exploratory played an important role at the time because I still had a strong connection to a logical, scientific mind. This exploratory into the quantum world from an amateur's perspective was enough to give me a sort of resolution at the time that there was a modest amount of compatibility between science and spirituality today and more is on the horizon.

Looking back from the perspective of today, I see how this exploratory deepened my spirituality. Everything was starting to come together. Where there had been a dichotomy, there was now unity of thought and understanding, at least from my perspective.

My wisdom inspired life took another step forward.....now with even more confidence that this was the right path for me.

TEN
CHAPTER

Mind, Body, Healing

I was on vacation with my family at Lake Tahoe, which is always our best vacation of the year. We have been going there in the summer for over two decades.

I began to feel pain in my left shoulder and arm. Products like Advil did little to relieve the pain. The pain increased each day and by the time we left I was consistently uncomfortable. After returning home and to work, the pain also continued its daily increase. I woke up one night about 2 AM in so much pain that I drove myself to the emergency room. After hours of waiting, I received a prescription pain medication, which did little to relieve the pain.

The next day I went to an orthopedic and later to a neurologist. They concluded the pain was because of two severely compressed discs in my neck. Relieving the pain would require very risky surgery that involved going through my throat to repair the damaged discs in my spine. (Of note, these compressed disks had existed for over two decades.) Until then they had me taking high potency narcotic pain medication, which only slightly dulled the pain.

During this two-week medical journey, I went to work for a few days. In a routine conversation with the account executive of our advertising agency, I mentioned my medical condition and the doctor's proposed solution. He quickly observed that he had a friend who had had a similar issue. This friend saw a doctor in New York and when he came back he was pain-free and no surgery had been involved. He offered to find out the name of the doctor.

When he called me the next day, he confirmed the previous information and indicated the doctor had written a book *Healing Back Pain: The Mind-Body Connection* by Doctor Sarno. I immediately ordered the book from Amazon for next day delivery. When it was delivered on a Friday, I immediately began to read it.

Very early in the book, I had a startling experience that changed my life. The book asked if there is a possibility that the mind could be the cause of the pain. I had read enough of Deepak Chopra's fascinating work by this time that I knew there was a mind and body connection. The book asked if it was "possible" and did not require the higher level of "knowing" that my pain was caused by my mind. As a result, I easily and quickly acknowledged that it was "possible."

At this exact instant, I heard an audible pop or miniature explosion like sound in my body. I immediately noticed that my pain had markedly dropped. Startled and confused best describes what I felt at that moment.

I read on in the book. It went on to say that if I could acknowledge the possible role my mind played in the pain, I might feel a "shift." Based on my experience, that was a major understatement. The book added that if I felt such a "shift" that I should immediately begin living my life as I had before the pain. What?

Instead of fighting or doubting, I embraced and engaged what I just read. I immediately stopped taking the prescription narcotic pain medication and started taking Tylenol (this lasted for a few days and then I stopped taking any pain medication). Since the book suggested I should begin living my life normally again, I went out running the next morning. I had not done this for weeks because of the pain. While the run was uncomfortable, it was doable and I resumed my normal running schedule.

A part of my normal workout schedule had also been working with some light weights. When I resumed this part of my work out, I quickly discovered that the muscles in my left arm had atrophied about 67% or a two-thirds loss in strength. I adjusted my weight schedule and over the next few weeks my left arm gradually returned to its pre-pain strength.

About a month after the startling experience of reading about the possibility that my mind could be the cause of my pain, I was pain-free and back to my old self.

While this remarkable process was going on, I kept one of my appointments with the neurologist who had recommended the risky surgery. He immediately rejected the possibility that what I had experienced was a long-term solution from the advice in the book. He pressed hard to convince me that surgery was the only long-term solution (something in me said he had a boat payment to make). On one level I was shocked and on the other level I understood. I was shocked because I was sitting in his office pain free and he still wanted to do high-risk surgery. I understood because he had no understanding of or belief in the mind – body connection. As I write this more than twenty years after this experience, that pain has never returned.

To put this experience in a broader context, this occurred during the same period that I was discovering psychics in the San Francisco area. I was still in the early waking up process (and still am). This experience acted as a powerful personal validation of how much we didn't know (this time, how much the medical community did not know), and that there was a world of awesome and inspiring potentialities. For me there was an undeniable, little understood (at least by the Western world) new reality waiting to be discovered. Now that's exciting!

My personal journal entry added an interesting perspective.

I would never have guessed that John (the advertising agency account executive mentioned earlier) *would be the "messenger" who connected me with the most remarkable healing experience of my life. I am glad I have begun to open up to new possibilities. A few years ago I probably would have ignored his story and not inquired further. I am not sure what this is all about but whatever it is, I am grateful!!!*

The next experience occurred about two years later.

The place for this next experience was not one where you would expect a remarkable life-healing event to occur. I was attending a week-long training session at the Center for Creative Leadership in San Diego. This was a weeklong training and self-awareness program that is one of the better ones.

There were 23 people in this week's program, and I had never met any of them before coming to the event. On the second day, we went outside for a trust building exercise. I was paired up with a woman whom I had not even said "hello" to so far. In this exercise she was blindfolded and my task was to guide her successfully through a maze. During this exercise, I guided her by putting my hands on her shoulders to help provide direction. We successfully navigated the maze in about 15 minutes.

On the evening of the fourth day the entire group went out to dinner. On the bus ride back to the hotel, the woman from the exercise sat next to me and asked if we could talk. It turned out it was so noisy on the bus that we waited until we got to the hotel lobby.

She then proceeded to tell me an amazing story. She had a very high level of neck and shoulder pain for over a decade. Doctors could not find its cause and so treated it with powerful prescription pain medication. There was not a day in over ten years that she did not live in pain. That is, until two days before when during the trust building exercise she found that her pain went away. She waited 48 hours to tell me to determine if the pain relief lasted. It had. For the first time in over a decade she was pain-free and felt that it was a direct result of my having guided her by putting my hands on her shoulders.

She asked me what I had done. I told her that I was clueless (a familiar feeling in my life). I told her that I had no special abilities and did not work in the healing field. During the exercise, my only purpose was to help her successfully make it through the maze.

I had a very emotional reaction to what she was telling me. I felt a tremendous sense of joy at the joy that I saw in her face. She was pain-free for the first time in over a decade. She was elated and deeply grateful.

Again, my personal journal entry illustrates my frame of mind at the time.

The tears are tears of joy. Just thinking about her healing makes me tear up again. As I sat and listened to her story it was like the only thing in this busy hotel lobby was her. Her story was the only thing I could hear. While it was a story I had never heard before either directly or indirectly, it strangely was not startling. Instead, it was this weird mix of "of course" and astonishment. Words are failing me here. Even as I read what I've just written, I realize the inadequacies of these words. There was no sense of ego, like "I did this?!" None. I felt only joy for her.

I talked to her six months later and she was still pain-free.

This was a powerful and remarkable experience and I did not like feeling clueless about what had just happened. I set out to learn.

I rather quickly discovered that there is a hands-on healing practice called reiki. Its apparent roots trace back a couple thousand years and there is a specific training program you can go through to develop hands-on diagnostic and healing capabilities.

Not surprisingly, I engaged and completed the three stage training program. The hands-on diagnostic process was particularly intriguing. In training with one of my teachers, I discovered a "warm spot" on her left knee as I did a hand scan of her body (warmth or heat are a sign of an area possibly needing some healing). At that time, she told me that she had no injury or anything wrong with her knee. A week later she called me and told me that her left knee had collapsed and probably required a surgical repair. She indicated that I had detected the weak spot in the exact place she was now needing surgery.

The hands-on healing process involves several detailed steps including use of specific symbols. Importantly, the actual healing has little to do with the person doing the healing. The healer's primary job is to create a clear channel for healing energy to flow through them to the person they are trying to help. The actual healing comes from energy flowing through the healer from an outside source.....God

The degree of healing is a function of the healer's ability to create a clear channel and the receptivity of the person they are trying to heal. Another important dimension is if the injury is related to a karmic event. If so, the healing process is very limited at best.

After I completed my training, I was left with the conundrum of what to with this. I still have not found a good answer. My primary purpose of completing the training was to gain understanding of what happened in San Diego. Now that I have this understanding, I've chosen not to use whatever ability I have since it does not seem to fit the specific life purpose that I appear to have. I occasionally wonder if there will be future opportunities that emerge to use what I've learned to serve others.

Since these two events occurred within a few years of each other, they significantly added to the series of revelations that were happening in many aspects of my life at the time. In combination with psychics, quantum physics, and wisdom-based spirituality (I'll talk about that shortly), doors were rapidly opening into a whole new world.

Deepak Chopra's books on the mind-body connection also made strong impressions on me during this period of time. As I was to discover later, this deep interest in healing lead to a later, very unexpected life-transforming event. This will be the subject of the next chapter.

The next powerful healing experience did not occur until about ten years later. It involved pain in my right shoulder and the upper part of my right arm. An MRI identified the cause as a bone spur in my right shoulder. I underwent some traditional medical treatment including a cortisone shot and some simple physical therapy. Despite this the pain level remained high and could spike to extremely high when I moved my arm in the wrong way. For example, twice I moved my arm in a manner that produced such a high level of pain that my knees buckled and I found myself on the floor doing deep breathing to relieve the pain. I reached a point where the doctor said, "The only way to relieve the pain is surgery on your right shoulder to remove the bone spur."

I delayed a decision on surgery for two reasons. First, we were moving into a new house and it would be helpful if I could assist with the lifting which would not be possible if I had surgery. Second, I decided to use the alternative healing process of visualization.

I began my visualizations immediately after a deeper than normal meditation. Since I had seen an MRI image of the bone spur, I knew exactly where it was in my shoulder. Using this information I visualized very specifically the "shaving" of the bone spur. I saw the "shaving" of electrons from the bone spur, reflecting my understanding that there was nothing solid, just an electromagnetic wave that needed to be adjusted. After three "shaving" visualizations that lasted about ten minutes each, I noticed a distinctly lower pain level in my shoulder.

At this point I stopped the visualizations to assess the results. A week later I discovered that I was pain-free and had a complete range of motion. There was not even a twinge of discomfort where there had been previously a pain level of 10 on a scale of 1-10. As I write this, it has been a little more than three years since that experience and my shoulder remains pain-free.

The only variable in my life during the brief period of "shaving" the bone spur was the visualizations. There was no change in diet, lifestyle, or exercise. Some of you reading this will believe that there must be some other cause. I understand that. Since I lived a few months with a level of pain that sometimes could make my knees buckle and land me on the floor doing deep breathing to relieve the pain, the before visualization and after visualization differences are dramatic. From a deep sense of inner knowing, I have no doubt that the visualizations removed the bone spur. Since the insurance company will not pay for another MRI to confirm this, we are left with the undisputable result.

My journal entry at the time reflects my state of mind when I realized I was pain-free.

> *I think I love being surprised. My visualizations were not done with complete confidence that they would work. Truth be known, I probably had more doubt than belief. What I think I learned is that the visualizations need to be very precise and specific. In addition, there needs to be an intense, laser like focus. Each time I could "feel" that I was making progress. It will be interesting to try this process again. As I write this there is a twinge of fear that I may not be able to replicate it because I'm missing some "magic" element that really made the difference.*

Two years later I developed a similar condition in my left shoulder. An MRI confirmed a bone spur plus a badly frayed bicep tendon. Again, the doctor said that the only way to eliminate the pain was to have surgery. After trying the same methodology that I had previously and failing to see any improvement, I scheduled surgery. This seemed to confirm by misgivings in the journal entry above; there was a "magic" element that I missed. Between the time I scheduled the surgery and the surgery date, I recalled an alternative healing process that can be best described as "injecting" some very high energy healing into the spot. Again, I did this in mediation over three separate occasions. After this the pain level had subsided 90% and I cancelled the surgery. I realized that the small level of residual discomfort was really the bicep tendon, not the bone spur. I then "injected" more healing energy into the tendon and it reduced it 90%. I am left with 99% less pain/discomfort.

These healing experiences served as powerful personal confirmations that the world is very different than I think it is and those differences represent some astounding possibilities. I was left with a great sense of wonder, awe, and deep, deep gratitude. From my readings, I knew that I was only at the very beginning of understanding this world of astounding possibilities. While you read a lot of "I" in this, I was only harnessing far greater powers than my ego could ever muster. The healing was not an "I" power but connecting to a greater power and allowing it to be present and work.

Just writing about these experiences reignites these powerful feelings that helped propel me to the next chapter in my life.

Taken individually each of these events was startling. Startling events are often unexpected and not understood, which is exactly what they were in the beginning. As the series of events unfolded I became increasingly knowledgeable and confident in what I was experiencing. It got to the point that I could replicate experiences using processes that I had experienced and learned about.

There is no doubt that my intuition spoke through these events in a compelling way that deepened and enriched my understanding of the world around me. The processes that I used came directly from a God realized teacher—Yogananda (a later chapter is devoted to telling more of this story). My intuition spoke through the events and He spoke through my teacher who helped me understand and utilize the new methods and insights. In many ways this was the most complete teaching I had received so far.

From the perspective of today, I see how this was the next logical step in my journey. Had I not developed the understandings from quantum physics about the body being an energy field and my spiritual practices, like meditation, I would never thought of trying to heal myself or anyone else. It also underscores how far I'd come on my journey up to this point. Contrasting the beginning point with Denise with these healing experiences, I see stark differences. From the beginning point I would've thought that anyone who talked about the kind of healing I experienced was delusional or just had a vivid imagination. These healing experiences gave me a front row seat to a world of possibilities that were now very, very real.

My wisdom inspired life was now in high gear......strong intuitive confirmation supplemented with real life demonstrations is a powerful transforming force.

What wonders will this next chapter hold?

ELEVEN
CHAPTER

Sogyal

Esalen was already a special place in my life even though I had only visited there three times before. From its location just south of Big Sur in California nestled on a cliff overlooking the Pacific, it provides a nurturing respite from the business life that dominated so much of my life during these days. Its famous hot springs were at beach level where you could overload your senses with a watery nirvana of sorts. A few yards in front of the hot springs Pacific waves crashed onto the shore while you experienced the hot springs' warming comfort.

After I moved from the eastern United States to California, I was able to visit more easily and frequently. Feeling the urge one day, I consulted their catalog to see what they offered on a particular weekend that I was available. Only one weekend workshop caught my attention because it was on "meditation and healing." I already had an interest in both topics so it seemed like a natural fit.

The teacher for this workshop was someone I had never heard of before and had a name that I had never encountered: Sogyal Rinpoche.

Despite my unfamiliarity with the teacher, I signed up for the weekend workshop primarily because of my interest in the topic.

When the Friday arrived for the start of the workshop, I made the two-hour drive to Esalen. After reaching Monterey, California, stunning views emerged for the rest of the drive down the Pacific Coast, to Big Sur with its tall redwoods, and finally Esalen. After checking in late in the afternoon, I went to my Spartan room that would be my home for the weekend.

The weekend workshop began at 7 p.m. Friday in a medium-sized room in one of the houses on the property. Almost twenty people waited for the session to begin. We all sat on pillows and beanbags. It was a group almost evenly divided between men and women and everyone was probably over the age of thirty-five.

Shortly after 7 p.m. Sogyal Rinpoche entered dressed in burgundy and yellow wraps. After a brief nod to the group and without any words he began to put a few items on a mantle behind where he was to sit. I later learned that these were pictures of his teachers who he held in high esteem.

Virtually everything about him was different than anything I'd ever seen. His dress was very casual and unpretentious. When he did begin to speak, he said nothing about himself. After confirming the topic with no elaboration and the Friday through Sunday meeting schedule, he asked each of us to introduce ourselves. In our introduction, he asked for each of us to note how experienced we were with meditation plus what our hopes were for the workshop.

Each of us introduced ourselves in traditional ways: name, job, where we lived and then added some mention of meditation experience and hopes for the workshop. At this time in my life I was still very much into my job defining who I was so I made a particular point of noting that I was a "vice president of marketing." Looking back, I can see that while I felt this was prestigious, for this particular group it probably made me a semi-outcast.

This first session lasted little more than an hour before we adjourned until Saturday morning. The Saturday and Sunday sessions lasted about two hours each morning and afternoon, with the afternoon sessions often being out in sunshine on the lawn overlooking the Pacific Ocean. He talked at each session without any notes on the topic of meditation from a number of different perspectives. Interestingly, he never directly talked about the topic of healing. When I asked him at the end of the last Sunday session why he had not discussed healing, he responded, "We did discuss healing." Only later did I realize that one of the powerful benefits of meditation is healing.

In my conversations with other group members I learned that "Rinpoche" is a title bestowed on highly advanced practitioners of Tibetan Buddhism. Some have referred to the title as the equivalent of a Ph.D. in Tibetan Buddhism. "Sogyal" was a name given to him when he was recognized as the reincarnation of a previous great Tibetan Buddhist master. Shortly after his birth, he manifested remarkable abilities that resulted in his recognition. At a very young age, he moved away from his parents to live in a monastic environment. Like others of his generation, he later experienced the trauma of the Chinese occupation of Tibet and the escape with the Dalai Lama from Lhasa over the mountains to India. His education continued in England where he developed great English-language fluency.

After this first weekend workshop on "meditation and healing," I returned to the same workshop over the next three years. The format and basic messages remained the same each year. The groups continued to be twenty or fewer people in a very informal, comfortable setting. The rest of the Esalen experience reinforced the spiritual like environment. The small running creek through the center of the property, the delicious vegetarian meals, the incredibly beautiful vegetable and flower garden, and a respect for quiet all made it a very special place to experience this great teacher.

So far, nothing I said would suggest that Sogyal Rinpoche is one of the most powerful, transformative figures in my life. He was and is exactly this for me. Describing what it is about him that is so powerful and attractive is very difficult. What is clear, is that after these modest workshop presences, Sogyal went on to become an international teacher, best-selling author of a seminal text on Tibetan Buddhism (*The Tibetan Book of Living and Dying*), and a highly respected figure in meetings between the Dalai Lama and leading Western scientists.

So what is it about him that so transformed my life? I will do my best to explain it, but it is one of those things for which words only tell part of the story. The most profound aspect of the experience is an inner sense and knowing that being with him contributed to changing the fundamental energy of my being.

Sogyal Rinpoche fundamentally redefined for me what a human being can be. Never before in my life had I encountered someone who was so wise and joyful. When he spoke, he awakened my inner knowing. Wisdom is inner knowing. When he spoke, I heard information for the first time. Instead of the reaction I have to new knowledge ("I never knew that before."), there was an inner sense of rediscovering or awakening to something I already knew. Something about his being....something about his energy was able to awaken my inner knowing.

The experience of being in his presence was so positive, so nourishing that the memory today immediately evokes a deep sense of gratitude. The experience was easy and profound. Each year as I returned, I was pleased to observe that my inner knowing seemed to open more easily and wider than it had the previous time.

While I do not recall many specific of his words of wisdom from these four workshops, I did clearly experience a transformation in the energy of my being. I knew that the rate of vibration of the energy in my being changed each time I was with him. The energy became calmer, more positive, and eventually more loving. While the changes were subtle, they were nonetheless profound and enduring.

Maybe the best way to put my experience is to observe that the greatest benefit was being in the presence of his energy. He was clearly the most spiritually evolved being I had ever been in the presence of at that time. It was like I was basking in the energy of his presence. Just as the sun can warm and comfort us, his energy evoked a transformative experience.

In the fourth year, we did a group meditation in which he said he would send us a blessing. I had no idea what this meant. We all sat in a semicircle in front of him and closed our eyes for the meditation. For the first time and for reasons I cannot explain, I decided to open my eyes during the meditation. What I observed stunned me. I saw concentric waves of energy emanating from him towards us. I immediately closed my eyes, rubbed them, and shook my head before reopening my eyes. When I did I saw exactly the same thing: waves of concentric energy emanating from him towards us. Bewildered, I closed my eyes and returned to the meditation. I then experienced one of the most positive meditations of my life.

A very special aspect of his presence was the joy that he exuded. Joy is one of those words that is sometimes confused with happiness, but it is much more than that. The dictionary defines joy as, "the emotion of great delight or happiness caused by something exceptionally good or satisfying; keen pleasure; elation." For most of us joy is an exceptional or very high level of happiness.

While a cliché does not do him justice, his smile would literally "light up the room." It was infectious to the point that you immediately felt the effect of more positive energy when he smiled. I found myself immediately smiling in response to his smile. At that time in my life a smile was almost a stranger in my life, so my smiling response to him was exceptional. It felt great!

Even more powerful than his smile was his laugh. His laugh came easily and abundantly. Like with his smile, I could not help but feel much better when he laughed.

One particular laugh is especially memorable. As background, Sogyal Rinpoche is often referred to as a Tibetan master. The title "master" refers to self-mastery, not any sense of mastery or authority over others. At the end of one of his sessions he indicated that students could purchase audiotapes of some previous presentations at a nominal cost. Methods of payment included cash or a credit card and then he paused. He then said, "Of course, you could use MasterCard." He first smiled and then laughed heartily. We all joined in.

As usual, my personal journal wonderfully reflected some of my feelings at the time.

> I look back in wonder. I chose to take the workshop with someone who had a name unlike anything I'd ever seen before. I went back year after year to take the same course from the same person in the same place. I had never done any of those things before. I am so glad that I did!

Before sharing a very special moment I had with Sogyal, I first need to provide an insight into what happened just before attending my fourth and last weekend session. The day prior to driving to Esalen, I visited with one of the few psychics I respected (in addition to Jose). At the end of a rather uneventful session, I was asked if I would accept a blessing. While I was not sure what this meant, how could I not accept something so seemingly unequivocally positive?

After saying "yes" I sat with my eyes closed not knowing what to expect. Suddenly I felt a strong tingling sensation at the crown of my head in the exact area I knew as my seventh chakra. It was the first (and so far only) time I had felt this. It was strong and sustained. It felt good, but strange. I stayed in the moment, suspending judging and just let it be.

While I do not know what the specific connection was to my time with Sogyal, I know they are connected. I have speculated that it brightened my aura in a way that he could see and while that may not be the specific connection I know that there is one. I feel it is connected to a special personal experience I had with him.

("Chakra" refers to the seven major energy centers running from the base of the spine to the crown of the head. And "aura" refers to our etheric or light body that can be seen by people with etheric vision......Barbara Brennan has some wonderful books on chakras and aura.)

It started when at the end of one of the sessions I went up to ask him a question. A couple of other students also had questions and when I tried to ask mine he told me to wait until the others were finished. While I am not a patient person, I did as I was told.

When he finished answering the other students' questions, he turned to me and told me to come with him. Before we started to walk, he reached out and took hold both of my hands. We then started to walk across the lawn leading to the overlook of the Pacific Ocean. It must have been a somewhat odd sight since I am 6'5" tall and he is about 5'3" tall. It was also strange because holding both hands and walking side by side is not a natural body position.

While today I do not recall any of the details of our conversation on that walk, I do remember feeling a deep sense of calm and connectedness with him. After our walk, I do recall walking to the vegetable and flower garden and being overwhelmed by the beauty of this garden that had the Pacific Ocean as a backdrop. I can also look back at the experience and see that it was the beginning of a new, rapid spiritual growth period in my life. The dimensions of this will become clearer in a couple of chapters. In rare situations when I share this story with others, I half jokingly say that he recognized me as the one student in the workshop who needed some industrial-strength help.

For more than a decade, I have felt a deep sense of gratitude for the opportunity to connect with him and the gifts he gave me. Each morning I get on my knees and express the following, "Sogyal Rinpoche, thank you for coming into my life and touching my life. You let me know what a human can be. Your compassion, wisdom, and joy inspire me every day of my life."

He completely redefined my potential as a human being. While I am millions of miles behind him on the spiritual path, his example inspires me everyday to take another step in his direction.

Since those experiences I have followed his career and writings with great interest. I have an extensive library of audiotape presentations he's made around the world. Several years after the last healing and meditation workshop, I attended another weeklong series of his teachings. By then his popularity had grown so that there were now more than 1,000 people at the workshop. The lack of personal connection and intimacy of the earlier Esalen workshops made this a less than satisfying experience. Today I continue to benefit from his great wisdom through his international bestselling book, *The Tibetan Book of Living and Dying*, and his YouTube video teachings.

I now also live in an area where there is another Rinpoche, Za Rinpoche. I occasionally attend his teachings primarily to bask in his energy. He was also very helpful in reviewing and advising me on a chapter of one of my previous books.

Through all of this experience with these great Tibetan Buddhist teachers, my inner knowing becomes richer and deeper with each experience. It is through an open and awakened inner knowing that God speaks. While words seem so inadequate in describing inner knowing, inner knowing is a deep sense of calm and quiet through which certainty and clarity emerge.

Through the certainty and clarity I can increasingly understand the essence of who we really are and the principles that should guide my journey going forward. It doesn't get much better!

Before meeting Sogyal, I had read in several wisdom texts that when the student is ready there would be a teacher. While I'm not capable of determining whether I was really ready, clearly a very powerful teacher emerged in my life. For me, being in his presence was the most nourishing learning I had ever experienced up until then. His writings and recorded teachings also helped but being in the presence of someone who exemplified a new human potential was a compelling teaching that continues to inspire and guide me.

Again, from the perspective of prior to beginning my spiritual journey, I would never have gone to a workshop taught by a Buddhist master. Never. In deciding to go to this workshop there was absolutely no resistance or difficulty in making the decision. There was a sense of "Wow, this could be interesting!" As I have noted previously, these experiences only underscored the very real change, even dramatic change that was going on in my life. Hallelujah!

Not surprisingly, my meditation practice has expanded from the original 15 minutes per day to 30–45 minutes. Sogyal's example and help made for richer and more rewarding meditations. Over the years I clearly experienced a calming in meditation that increasingly carried over into my everyday life. I look back on those early years of meditation, and am both proud and a bit surprised that I was so dedicated and committed to everyday practice. The chattering mind was and is still enemy number one, and probably will be for the rest of my life. Having said that, the calming and deepening of my awareness that I experience from meditation is profoundly beneficial.

My intuition made it very clear I was in the presence of a very wise teacher. His presence further opened my inner knowing. My intuition spoke through him in ways that became increasingly compelling and clear. From the perspective of today, I can see that this channel was barely open at the time. I also strongly suspect that from the perspective of the future the same will be said about the current openness of this channel. That is a thrilling prospect!

Looking back I realize that my intuition spoke in a way that importantly filled in a critical gap in my journey. So much of what I had done before studying with Sogyal was intense learning and experiences. Each made a powerful impression, many of which inspired me to live a better life; a better life in accordance with the new insights that come into my life. But this experience was intensely personal and spiritual. Psychics/channels had been personal but the spirituality paled in comparison to my times with Sogyal. For the first time, I had direct personal experience with a human being who completely redefined what a human could be. Thank you, God.

TWELVE
CHAPTER

Ignorance & Learning

Maybe I did not know everything, but what I did not know was not worth knowing. Prior to the experience with Denise, I would've said something like this and believed it.

One of the big changes along this journey is the positive recognition of how ignorant I am. Recognizing my ignorance has completely changed my relationship with the world around me. The more I learned, the more ignorant I realized that I was.

The impetus of this recognition has been to launch me into a world of learning. Its major manifestations are reading, teaching, and writing. I have already addressed how reading has inspired and changed my life. I have to be one of Amazon's best customers since I read 25 – 50 books a year.

Teaching became a completely unexpected part of my life. When I moved to Arizona for the second time after leaving Gallo in the late 1990s, I guest lectured a few times at Arizona State University's West campus. Shortly after my last guest lecture, the head of the marketing department called me and asked me if I was interested in teaching. I said, "No." He asked if I would at least talk to him about the opportunity. Since he had been kind enough to invite me as a guest lecturer, I felt that I owed him at least a brief chat on the topic.

When I showed up at his office that same day, he put a course schedule for the coming semester in front of me and asked what courses I would like to teach. While at Procter & Gamble I had been a successful sales manager, and I recognized this as one of the most assumptive attempts to sell that I had ever experienced. He clearly was ignoring my unambiguous statement that I had no interest in teaching.

I decided to play along with him. After a few questions about specific courses, I pointed to three different courses that I would teach if I were interested. This was enough for him. He then invited me to walk with him to the office of the dean of the school of management. I had never met him before and I immediately recognized that he was a fairly strong introvert.

After a very brief welcome from him, he asked me, "How much would you like to be paid?"

"Paid to do what?" I responded.

"Teach these courses," he said as he pointed to the three courses marked in the course schedule.

For some strange reason I found myself saying, "This is an entirely new thought to me. I have done no research on the topic." I paused for a moment, looked at him intently, and then said, "I am going to trust you to pay me what is right." It was almost as if someone else were speaking.

He reflected for a moment and then gave me an annual salary figure.

Even to this day I am shocked that the next thing I said was, "Yes."

Less than four hours before saying this, I had not considered teaching at any level at any time in my life. Now I found myself agreeing to become a full-time faculty member in the school of management, complete with my own office.

Stranger still are the following facts. First, I never filled out an application for the job. Second, at the time I was not even sure that they had a resume, although I learned later that they did. Third, my only degree was a bachelor of arts in prelaw. I had never taken any of the courses I had just agreed to teach. While I did not have the educational background to qualify for teaching these courses, I certainly had the years of experience and success in business (the real world for the topics I was to teach) to qualify.

I would later learn that the sum total of my experience was the equivalent (according to their system) of a PhD without the dissertation.

Looking back at this hiring experience, I can only conclude that there was some larger force at work here. In the spirit of this book, my intuition spoke, I listened, and found myself agreeing to do something that I had never considered doing as either a part or full-time job before in my life.

I proceeded to teach full-time for two years and part-time (one course per semester) for four years. For the entire six years I always taught management and leadership courses. I always found it interesting that of all the people teaching these courses, I was the only person who had led anyone at any time in the real world.

I taught my students from a very practical perspective. After my first semester of teaching with the generally accepted $100 textbook, I switched the required reading to books like Stephen Covey's *Seven Habits of Highly Effective People* and Blanchard's *One Minute Manager*. Apparently my students appreciated my practical and passionate approach to teaching. My student ratings were consistently higher than other people teaching the same or similar courses, despite the fact that the average grade was a full grade point lower than what other teachers awarded their students.

Teaching is learning. I discovered the truth in the age-old adage that "the best way to learn something is to teach it." Learning occurred along multiple dimensions. First, I deeply learned the substantive material I was teaching about how to be a great leader in business and life. The comprehensiveness of the material continually reminded me of the complexities and challenges associated with being a great leader. I taught what I believed in and what worked for me in the real world. While I did not bring my spiritual path into the classroom, I did bring many of its fundamental principles like integrity, compassion, and doing the right thing even when it was the most difficult thing to do.

Second, I more deeply learned some lessons about my ability to help people. Students engaged my courses with a range of motivations, ranging from wanting to get the course checked off a list (about 90% of students) all the way up to wanting to sincerely be a very good leader. Each semester I relearned the lesson that I could only really help those who wanted to be helped. I learned to never be frustrated by people who did not want to be helped by the material in the course. I respected where they were coming from. On the other hand, those who wanted to be helped (a distinct minority) were a joy to work with. As they engaged the material they shared their personal experiences that brought the lessons to life in ways I could not have imagined. In these ways, they taught me.

Third, I learned about the challenges of our educational systems. For the most part, these were not positive learnings. Based on my experience, academics give lip service to the importance of being a great teacher. They reserve their greatest positive energy for research and the academic politics required for career progress.

Separately, the system uses one fundamental teaching model for almost every course, which is a lecturer with overheads or PowerPoint slides. While this helps to impart information, it does little to help students engage the material and to explore, very importantly, it's personal relevance and application. My extensive efforts to have broad-based dialogue in every class served to be a poor to moderately successful approach to help students get the greatest value from the transmitted material.

Unfortunately, my teaching experience did not reveal any major new insights about how to fundamentally fix a flawed teaching model. On the subject of leadership, my work as an executive coach was far more effective as a teaching model since the material was always personally relevant and involved immediate action steps in their real world. It's not clear to me that this model translates well from a one-on-one environment to a 30 − 40 student environment.

Another major learning dynamic for me is writing books. Prior to this book, I authored five books, three published (before teaching at ASU) by significant publishers and two self-published books. In addition, there are a few written but unpublished books. What most of these have in common is that they were initiated because of my deep desire to learn and contribute to a topic of significant personal interest. I would become deeply curious about a topic, engage in deep learning, and attempt to contribute something new and meaningful to a topic. The deep learning and creation of a book often took at least six months and sometimes more than a year.

My first attempt at writing a book was motivated by my spiritual journey. At the time, there were numerous books about the soul and for the most part I found them confusing and incomplete based on the learning path I was on. Feeling that the soul was an exceptionally important topic, I set out to write the best book about the soul. My working title was "OH Joyous Soul." I drew upon many sources with a special emphasis on the Ageless Wisdom, which I discuss in a couple of chapters.

After finishing it, I shared the book with a friend who had a published book to his credit. He provided generally positive feedback, but suggested that my writing needed to be significantly improved. I hired an editor that he suggested and I learned from his improvements. I read books on how to get a literary agent and sent off letters to many of them. I quickly learned to not be sensitive about rejection, especially since every literary agent rejected my proposal for this book. I put it aside thinking that maybe its time had not yet come.

My next inspiration came early on a Friday evening as I was listening to NPR. They mentioned that it was Leo Durocher's birthday and that his autobiography was titled *Good Guys Finish Last*. My immediate reaction was, "No! Good guys finish first." I quickly decided to write a book with the working title of *Nice Folks Finish First*. At the time I made this decision, I was driving to our house in the mountains. That weekend I completely sketched out the book's outline and within a week had started to identify people who would become part of the book. My intent was to write about people who were good, caring human beings and very successful in business. At the time, people like "chainsaw Al Dunlap" were being glorified for their business results despite an almost inhumane treatment of the people in a company.

The first person I approached for the book was Joe Mansueto, the founder of Morningstar, and he quickly agreed to the extensive set of interviews needed to be part of the book. How could he resist? My approach said, "I identified in my research that you are a good, caring human being who clearly has been very successful in business. I am writing a book to let people know that nice folks can finish first. Would you like to be part of delivering this message?" Everyone I had the opportunity to ask agreed to be part of the book.

It was a joy to write. I learned so much about the richness of the human spirit. When I began the book, I did not personally know of too many real life examples. When I finished the book, my faith in the nice folks finish first leadership model had risen to a level of deep belief in its power and benefits. The ten people in the book inspired me and motivated me to want to share their stories with others.

Unfortunately, that proved far more difficult than I imagined. Again, 100% of the literary agents I solicited rejected the opportunity to represent this book. They indicated that as a first-time author publishers were reluctant to support my message and work.

Then something powerful happened. At the time I said that, the Universe wanted to see this book published based on what happened next. Two unexpected calls solved my problem. Today, I recognize this as another example of the Universe speaking through others and making opportunities available that I acted upon to achieve my objectives.

First, as I was digesting the final rejections, I received a call from one of the literary agents who had turned me down. She indicated that the publisher of the Idiot books (Macmillan) was doing a national search for an author to write about five minute managing. She knew I had been in business and wondered if I would be willing to submit my resume for consideration. I agreed and a few weeks later I was told I had been selected. I was more than a little bit surprised because nothing in my résumé suggested any knowledge about five minute managing. Based on this I could only conclude that the one criterion I did fit was being an idiot.

My outline for the book was accepted with no changes. I quickly embarked on researching and writing the book. In rather short order my manuscript was accepted and the book moved forward to publication as *The Complete Idiot's Guide to Five Minute Managing*.

Second, one week after that manuscript was accepted, another agent who had rejected my nice folks book called and asked if I would be interested in being a co-author and finishing a book that was 40% complete. Since I had considerable knowledge and experience on the subject matter, I agreed. With a minimum of research and calling upon my extensive experience, this book was also completed in a relatively short period of time. It was published as *By the Numbers*.

Since the number one objection to my nice folks book had been that I was only a first-time author, I now re-approached literary agents with two published books to my credit. I was now searching for an agent to represent what would be my third published work. I quickly secured an agent who then sold it to a publisher. The publisher titled the book *The New Wisdom of Business* and later had it published in China and Germany.

Amazing AND true.

My next book flowed directly from my spiritual journey. As I progressed down the path I could not help but notice that I was becoming happier. I also recognized that happiness was a powerful positive force in my life and wondered how I could become even happier.

I dove into the topic and quickly discovered that there were books on happiness from a Western perspective and other books from an Eastern perspective. I did not find one book that did an excellent job of combining these perspectives. I quickly determined that producing such a book could make a major contribution to a very important topic. That was the genesis of *Ultimate Happiness, Best Proven Western & Eastern Insights About How to be Happier Today*.

My research included a twenty-two week course led by Dr. Marty Seligman, the founder of the field of positive psychology. The emergence of this field and his trailblazing work into happiness from a Western science perspective is a major contribution. His initiative has resulted in numerous other Western researchers to add significant contributions to our understanding about what we can do to be happier.

From an Eastern perspective my research focused on the Buddhist and Self Realization Fellowship insights into personal happiness. My work was helped by the contributions of Za Rinpoche and a senior monk in the Fellowship.

The researching and writing of this book significantly advanced my understanding of how to become personally happier day by day. After completing the book and having my proposal rejected by all the literary agents I solicited, I decided the book was too important to go unpublished. My proposal was rejected because I lacked formal credentials in the field, which would be very important to potential readers. I self published the book but with little financial and marketplace success. The lack of financial success was totally unimportant, but I was disappointed that a very practical and important book would fail to help the millions of people who could benefit from it. This disappointment aside, the book had great learning value for me; a value that is appreciated everyday.

The book before this one is also one that I am passionate about and that I learned major insights in the course of researching and writing it. Its working title is *WE Power, version 3.0, The Death of Command and Control Management*. There are already two very successful versions of empowered management that in some cases is management without bosses. This approach has succeeded in both very large and small businesses across a variety of industries. In my opinion, it is the future of leadership and management.

While it has been successful, the transition today from command-and-control management to "we power" is long and uncertain. In writing this book, I point out several highly successful processes used in different contexts that when applied to transitioning management can greatly accelerate the speed and certainty of success.

Again, this is another process where my learning curve was often pointing north. I felt that I had successfully processed my extensive learning to create new insights and methods. Based on the rejection again by literary agents of my proposal to publish this book, I think it may be another case where I am a bit too far into the future with this book. I deeply believe that its time will come.

From the perspective of my life journey so far, I have traveled from a high level of arrogance and blindness that led me to thinking I knew far more than I did to a deep and wonderful appreciation of how ignorant I am. This appreciation led to a life of continuous learning. Today the majority of the learning focuses on relearning and relearning yet again major spiritual insights, primarily from the Yogananda's Gita commentary.

Learning is now addictive in its most positive sense. What and how I learn seems to be guided by my intuition dropping inspiration into my awareness and bringing people and opportunities into my life that stimulate my curiosity. For all of this, I am deeply grateful. This is another wonderful dimension of a wisdom inspired life.

THIRTEEN
CHAPTER

Creativity

Wisdom unlocks higher levels of creativity.

Creativity seems to be one of the things that I'm best at. At least it would appear that way based upon what I find easy and fun to do.

During many of the years covered by the chapters so far, I have worked in the field of creativity. The secondary manifestation has been in the books I have researched and written. My primary focus has been helping large companies invent new products. Over the years, I've developed a model and process that probably does this better than any other company. It is my primary work as I write this book.

Having said that, I have frequently questioned why my spiritual path has not led me to serve a more noble purpose than helping companies sell more food, paper, or bank accounts. I have been truly open to that possibility and have often proactively searched for that noble purpose but without much success to date. Again, I trust that when and if using my creativity skills to serve a more noble purpose is right that I will be able to see it.

In helping companies invent new products I have developed a process that appears almost magical when you see it at work. In part, it is because the process is built on principles that tap into higher personal abilities and connects people in ways that facilitate quick, high quality connections.

One of the critical principles is to bring together a highly diverse and talented group of people. The dimensions of diversity include functional expertise, kinds of real-world experience, a rich cultural mix, and a variety of interests and motivations. When we work with a company in a two or three day creative session, the majority of people in the session are from outside the company. Companies typically want "out-of-the-box" ideas and it is impossible to get those kinds of ideas from people that only live in the box.

This high-quality diversity helps leverage a second critical principle, which is the introduction of stimulus into the creative process. Stimulus gets people looking at opportunities and objectives in ways they would not normally relate to them. Typically, stimulus is provocative in ways that create new to the world, practical solutions.

The third critical principle in our process is to reduce fear among people generating creative ideas. Reducing fear becomes critical to success because the big ideas often start as outrageous, wild and wacky ideas that quickly become transformed into powerful, practical ideas. People need to be fearless about being able to be outrageous if the process is to succeed.

The fourth critical principle is that left and right-brained people are equally creative, both quantitatively and qualitatively. We know this from scientific studies that destroy the myth that only certain people are creative or that only right brain people are truly creative. Having said that, left and right brain dominant people create ideas in very different ways. We know the differences and tailor idea generating exercises to the unique profile of people directly involved in the creative process.

Enough of this microanalysis of creativity!

Probably one of the greatest reasons supporting creativity success is the recognition of my high level of personal ignorance. In the previous chapter, I pointed out that this insight propelled me down the road of learning.

When I started working in the area of creativity, my ignorance prevented quick judgment and unlocked playing with possibilities. Since the process purposely involved people with very high levels of diverse expertise, it made the suspension of judgment and playing with possibilities one of the most fun and productive experiences of my life. The process of combining the brilliant ideas of many into even bigger ideas is almost magical. My dedication to learning and respect for diversity helped me to facilitate the creative success of others.

My professional focus on creativity flows to every other part of my life. I seek out diverse expertise in a variety of topics and use the learning to play with creative possibilities. While at some point engaging the discriminating mind is both helpful and necessary, the period of disengagement is far more productive and helpful than I ever imagined possible.

So much of my wisdom journey has and continues to be guided by a spirit of imagining possibilities, many of which I am in the process of bringing to life.

FOURTEEN
CHAPTER

My Heart Opens

I really felt my heart. There was no pain but it was clearly the energy focal point in my body. It had a distinct, undeniable center stage presence in my consciousness.

At the time, I was watching car after car drive up to the Modesto, California, Red Cross offices to make donations. The donations had been arriving for several days in a steady stream from early morning and into early evening. People really wanted to help their fellow residents impacted by the 100 year floods (mid 1990s) in our community. It was more than just the physical act of donating. Donating was an important manifestation of the attitude present in everyone who donated. The attitude was, "I care. I want to help."

Looking back, I now understand better what was happening. For days, I had been around people who opened their hearts and acted in the best way they thought possible to help their fellow citizens. The cumulative power of being around that energy had powerfully, undeniably, and permanently opened my heart.

For me this meant that for the first time I understood the meaning of compassion that had been so powerfully taught to me by Sogyal. Even in that moment, I knew that I wanted to compassionately serve others. It felt SO RIGHT. There have been very few times in my life that I was aware of a major shift happening in my life at the moment it was happening. This was one of those. As time passed this initial awareness grew into a commitment and a search for ways of acting on it.

My association with our local Red Cross chapter started several years earlier. This vague feeling of wanting to give back something to my community developed and I searched for ways to act on it. Initially it led to a chamber of commerce leadership program introducing me to many of the key government and organizational leaders. While that did not lead to any specific action plan, I later learned that Gallo's senior management was strong supporters of the Red Cross. One of the executives had been on the board of the local chapter and was leaving which created an opportunity for me. This began a several year association. The first several years were focused on dramatically improving the economics of the chapter. This was highly successful and resulted in building a new chapter office and having a sustainable economic model that eliminated much of the year-to-year financial uncertainty.

I gradually increased my role and eventually became head of the Board of Directors for the chapter. We had an exceptional chapter manager who made the directors' jobs easy. The chapter significantly expanded the range of services provided to the community and invested heavily in training people who would then go to disaster areas when the national chapter called upon them. Overall, the chapter became a top performer in the Red Cross system.

About five years into my association with the chapter, we had massive flooding in our community due to a combination of very heavy rain on top of a mountain snowpack. This broke levees and caused excessive water to be released from a major dam. It became our turn at the 100-year flood. We quickly became a disaster that the national chapter took charge of and brought people in around the country to supplement the relatively small group we had in our chapter.

At the peak of activity, I left my job on most days to work at the chapter in whatever capacity the director needed. At first it was getting more phone lines into the chapter to handle the dramatic increase in calls for help and offers of help. It then moved to a wide variety of tasks to handle the massive inflow of physical and financial donations. It later grew to coordinating activities with other agencies like the Salvation Army and governmental groups. Once the intense activity subsided, I returned to a more modest brief daily involvement over the next couple of months.

While the work was challenging and time-consuming, I found it was very energizing. Even after a long day, I felt uplifted and extremely gratified at the opportunity to help others. Towards the end of the crisis, I had a strange feeling of disappointment that the intense activity was ending. It felt so good to be helping others that I did not want to end.

I immediately began looking for more opportunities to help, but realized that what I had just experienced was very unusual (it was a 100 year flood after all). I deepened my involvement and commitment to the chapter and looked more broadly in the community for opportunities. I did not find any.

As time passed, I remained alert to opportunities. I explored a few ideas only to find that they were more administrative and mundane than the frontline helping of others I craved.

About a year later, I realized that I did not have to look far for opportunities to act compassionately; opportunities to help relieve the suffering of others. I had the opportunity every day with people at work, friends, and family. While I will address the subject from a work perspective in a later chapter, it ultimately led to wanting to be a "servant leader." Managing from this perspective let me to actively address service opportunities by what became my mantra when interacting with others, "How can I help you?"

My heart had been so powerfully opened by the compassionate actions of others now became a daily guiding light in my interactions with virtually everyone in my world. The change was dramatic. Before opening my heart I had a very egocentric, self-serving philosophy. After opening my heart, I increasingly became less concerned about my own needs and more concerned about the needs of others and how I could help them.

Again, God spoke. I found myself in a powerful life situation, very different than anything I had experienced before, and fortunately I chose to listen. I listened to that very strong heart centered energy, felt its powerful influence, stayed focused, and finally acted to continue the presence of this energy well beyond the initial triggering experience.

From the perspective of today, I am so grateful this event came into my life. It truly opened my heart to the needs of others and that opening as continued to widen and deepen my commitment to serving others.

Wisdom inspires compassion. Wisdom inspires serving others. My wisdom inspired life was now in action beyond myself.

FIFTEEN
CHAPTER

Ageless Wisdom

Awesome and overwhelming.

These were the first two feelings I had when I first realized the full scope of more than twenty volumes of revelation called the Ageless Wisdom. It is not clear to me where I first heard about this series, but I do know that once I sampled a compendium volume titled *Ponder on This* that I immediately knew I needed the entire series.

The Ageless Wisdom is more than 10,000 pages of revelation transmitted by a great Tibetan master, Djwhal Khul, to an advanced devotee, Alice Bailey. The method of communication was mental telepathy. Given the highly evolved status of the Tibetan master the method of communication was very much like an advanced psychic (Alice) channeling a high-level source.

My simple description for the Ageless Wisdom has always been that it is the science of spirituality. It is all about the science of energy and the universal laws governing that energy.

The titles of some of the volumes are daunting: *A Treatise on Cosmic Fire, Esoteric Psychology, Esoteric Healing, The Rays and the Initiations,* and *A Treatise on White Magic*. Even more daunting is the writing. Sentences can run for an entire page or more. The vocabulary is new and complex. It is not easily digested reading, so much so that I have had to read some of the major volumes several times to get to a point of even modest understanding.

So why is something so difficult, so important?

It's importance rises from the subject matter, which is the spiritual science about how the world works. In all of my exploring I never found anything as comprehensive.

Here is a very brief sampling of the forward thinking insights from the Ageless Wisdom.

- Medical science: While acknowledging that we will continue to need doctors, surgeons, and hospitals for some time (in spite of their mistakes and faulty diagnosis), we will gradually move from addressing symptoms to real causes. One of the first steps will be a focus on the etheric body (visible to people that can see auras). The physical body's dependence on the etheric body will eventually lead to magnetic healing and vibratory stimulation replacing the present methods of surgery and drugs.
- The Plan: This refers to the Divine plan for our planet. The Ageless Wisdom says, "This next development of the Plan will produce in man an understanding – intelligent and cooperative – of the divine purpose for which the One in Whom we live and move and have our being, has deemed it wise to submit to incarnation." It goes on to counsel that only people who are fairly advanced along the spiritual path can begin to see and understand this Plan.
- Crime: The Ageless Wisdom points out the obvious fact that force and drastic penalties have not been very successful in preventing crime or deterring people from violent selfishness. Looking to the future it says, "The old methods must give way to the new, and the conservative attitude must be dropped in favor of religious, psychic, and physical training and experiment, scientifically applied, and mystically motivated. When I say religious, I do not refer to doctrinal and theological teaching. I mean the cultivation of those attitudes and conditions which will evoke reality in man, bring the

inner spiritual man in the foreground of consciousness, and thus produce the recognition of God."

- Spiritual man: "The spiritual man is he, having been both a man of the world and occult student, has reached the conclusion that behind all those causes with which he has been hitherto engaged is a CAUSE; this causal unity then becomes the goal of his search."
- Sex: "The belief that to be a disciple necessitates a celibate life, and complete abstinence from all natural functions, is neither correct nor desirable."
- Time: "The spiritual man is not conscious of time, once he is separated from the physical body.... There is no such thing as time on the inner planes, as humanity understands it. There are only cycles of activity or of non-activity."
- Telepathy: "It is necessary...to enter into telepathic rapport. This may seem to you to be a wonderful but impractical vision. I assure you that this is not so. The work of establishing this rapport may indeed be slow, but it is an inevitable effect of the growing sensitivity of all the souls who are working in the field of the world. The first indication of it is that instinctive recognition of those who constitute part of this group when they meet and contact each other in ways of the world intercourse. There comes to them an immediate flashing forth of the light, and instantaneous electrical interplay, a sudden sensing of a similarity of vision and, of objective, or a vital opportunity to aid in and to cooperate with each other in the work in which it is realized that all are interested."

I have shared some of the more straightforward guidance from the 10,000 pages. If you are just becoming interested in the spiritual path, this may not be the easiest and best point of entry onto this path. If you are intrigued, the compendium volume titled *Ponder On This* could be a good introduction for you.

The Ageless Wisdom was written from the early to mid 1900s. Since then there have been a few who have continued to openly teach and champion the revelation from this series. One of the most interesting is Benjamin Crème. Besides his connection to an advocacy of the Ageless

Wisdom, he has been openly predicting for decades the emergence of the world teacher who will be known as Maitreya. Through his magazine, Share International, he regularly publishes his belief that a world teacher is currently among us and will soon emerge to lead the world through the major challenges that it currently faces. Throughout history, there has been no shortage of people claiming either to be a prophet or predicting the emergence of one. Through my more than twenty-year casual association with his teachings I have had many mixed feelings.

Everything I have said so far about the Ageless Wisdom suggests that I have completely accepted its truth and accuracy. I am sure that many people may find this hard to accept. Please consider that leading up to this time I had had multiple positive experiences with psychics where I was able to personally verify the accuracy of the information. Also I had made considerable progress in developing a sense of inner knowing. While I did not make many personal journal entries about the Ageless Wisdom, this one reflects what I was experiencing at the time.

> When I read the AW there is a deep sense that I am reading truth. I have no external source of verification, but my own deep inner sense is one of seeing the world as it really is and a strong sense of gratefulness. The word "resonates" is the best that I can come up with our vocabulary today. This is very different than the sense of hopeful wishing that it is true. And strange as it sounds, there is a sense that I am rediscovering something I have known previously rather than learning something completely new. It feels very comfortable.

While there have been many books and teachers that have helped me on my journey that I am not mentioning, the Ageless Wisdom and Ken Wilber have been two of the more influential. Ken is one of the biggest thinkers on the planet today. I have studied his work on and off for a couple of decades. When I first started, understanding was hard to come by for me.

He has a remarkable big picture capability. He integrates all of the major teachings for centuries into a big picture view. From this view we see how so many lesser teachers (teachers looking at a smaller parts of the whole) are right from their unique perspective and how their insights connect with and relate to the teachings of others. It is truly a remarkable contribution he has made. His four-quadrant view of the world along with lines and stages of development provide a uniquely practical and powerful way to understand our world. Increasingly he has expanded his influence to leading edge thinkers in politics, economics, and social policy. He has published many books and for someone who is interested in an introduction, his latest books are among some of the most helpful. Deepak Chopra expresses very high regard for Ken's many contributions.

I want to share one more experience that has some links to the Ageless Wisdom. As mentioned previously, Benjamin Crème, an Englishman, has for the last few decades suggested that a great master will emerge into broad awareness on the planet in this time of tremendous need. While this great master will first be known as the great teacher, eventually we will know him as the Maitreya. Ben also has strong links to the Ageless Wisdom and sees it as one of the greatest contributions from the masters in recent times.

For several decades I have been a regular jogger. At the time of this event, I usually jogged at 4:30 AM. One cool summer morning while I was living in California, I went out as usual for my jog. The eastern sky was bright suggesting that the sunrise was not far away. I turned onto one of the streets that I regularly jogged on. It has tall trees on both sides of the street leaving a fairly narrow view of the eastern sky ahead.

This particular morning when I looked at the sky ahead, I saw a very distinctively shaped cloud that fit exactly into the narrow view I had. It quickly dawned on me that the cloud was a perfectly shaped cardinal bird.... and I do mean perfectly shaped. It was not one of those clouds that you look at and with some imagination can see a particular shape. The unique sharp angles of the head were perfect. There was a small hole in the cloud exactly where the eyes should be....there was some special cloud texture exactly where the wings should be. There was not even a wisp of an extraneous cloud element. The entire cloud was in the shape.

I stopped jogging and stared in amazement. I ingrained into my memory exactly what I was seeing. It was perfectly shaped.....it was perfectly positioned in the very small portion of sky that I could see.....it was beautifully lit by the brightening dawn sky. It was perfect. I thought of running home to get my camera but realized that would take too long.

In Ben's magazine, Share International, readers share unusual encounters and experiences, asking if they were with a master or generated by a master. In every issue Ben provides answers after consulting with a great, unnamed master. Since I was intensely curious about this very unusual encounter while I was jogging, I wrote him a letter asking for any perspective that he had.

In a later issue, after consulting with his master, he said Jesus manifested the cloud image of the cardinal bird. I was stunned and did not know if I believed him. I still don't know whether I believe him......but what I do know beyond a shadow of a doubt is that in that early California morning, I did see a cloud in the perfect shape of a cardinal bird. The potential spiritual meaning that a "cardinal" bird has is not lost on me, but the meaning of this event is still a mystery.

There are two other experiences that occurred while jogging early in the morning, both of these are UFO experiences. As background, the same Benjamin Crème mentioned above discusses UFOs extensively indicating that they are real, most come from Venus and Mars, and they are here to help us, often with the serious environmental and pollution challenges our planet faces. Again, I have no sense of inner knowing or other perspective that validates or invalidates his information.

The first experience happened early one January morning when I had moved to Arizona (late 1990s). It was a chilly morning and the skies were full of stars. After reaching the halfway mark of my run and starting my return, I gazed up at a small mountaintop only about quarter-mile mile from where I was running. I saw four lighted objects flying in the vicinity of the peak. I slowed down and then stopped to watch them for more than five minutes. My mind went through a process of trying to answer the question "what is this?" In short order I determined that it was not a group of helicopters, because they were flying to closely together and their quick, sharp angled turns were impossible for a helicopter to make. For many of the same reasons, I determined it was not a plane of any kind. It was an unidentified set of flying objects. The key word is "unidentified." I know what they were not, but do not know what they were.

The second experience happened about fifteen months later. I was nearing the end of my run early in the morning as the eastern sky was in the early stages of dawn. Suddenly in front of me, I saw a bright object crossing from right to left. My instant thought was that it was a meteor, but this clearly proved to be wrong. I stood and watched it for almost 2 minutes. What I saw was a brilliant, super white glowing object about the size of a small car. It was less than a quarter-mile in front of me and no more than 75 feet off the ground. It moved at a rate of about 1 mph on a level path. No meteor moves this slowly and parallel to the ground. I saw that it was heading towards a hill and wondered what would happen as it got closer. My answer was that it disappeared in a flash; it went out as fast as when you flip the switch for a light bulb. I was shocked. The glowing, almost throbbing white mass of light had no afterglow or even a dim remnant. Throughout this there was no sound. The path it took was over the rooftops of several houses. Again, I know what it was not, that is, a meteor. I can only call it an unidentified flying object.

While the first experience with the cloud has some possible meaning, the two UFO experiences remain a mystery. The best I can surmise is that these experiences were intended to give me firsthand glimpses into new elements of the reality around me. To that extent they did support and confirm my belief that the world is a very different place than we think it is. For that I am very grateful.

My intuition spoke by bringing the Ageless Wisdom and Ken Wilber's work into my awareness.

Out of millions of books a very, very few come into my awareness. During this period of my journey, the "normal course" of my life was business, business, and more business. It consumed most of my time and energy. For teachers and books to break through this focus was remarkable.

Books like the Ageless Wisdom (20+ volumes!) and Ken Wilbur's many books come into my awareness for a reason. There is a certain "meant to be" part of this reason, which I experience when I am aware of my reaction to a book. That reaction includes the feeling the first time I see or touch the book all the way through reading the book (this feeling started with Living with Joy). When I have a feeling of comfort and even gratitude for the experience, I am sure there is a strong connection that was meant to be. This "meant to be" energy is powerful enough to intervene in the "normal course" of my life.

Again, it is difficult for me to imagine that I would have noticed, looked for, or read any of these books if the events of previous chapters had not occurred. One event led to another…and led to another. At times I sensed there was a plan…and whenever this occurred I became excited about the future….what's next?!

God clearly knew that I needed help. By this time, I also knew I needed help. I was looking for help….and help came my way in the form of books, teachers, and a wide variety of people. I sometimes have the feeling that when my intuition spoke the message was, "Pay attention to this." Since so many unexpected and unusual forms of help have already arrived in my life, my openness to more unexpected and unusual help has become rather high.

Most of the books I read during this time (and there were many, many books) were helpful to modestly helpful. Most of these addressed parts of the big picture, like the importance of being present. In this chapter I have shared two major sources for me that were especially beneficial because of their big picture perspective.

The excitement of these events is clearly consistent with a wisdom inspired life. Wisdom developed an inspired purpose.

SIXTEEN
CHAPTER

Brief Pause And Reflection

About two decades after my first experience with the psychic Denise, I sat on Pfeiffer State Beach in Big Sur. Over the years I came here many times for a variety of purposes. This time it was to sort out some thoughts on where I had been and where I was going.

It was a perfect place to do this because I seemed to be fully alive when I was there. Waves crashed onto the shore. They reared up, accelerated to the beach, and pummeled the sandy beach. I smelled and almost thought that I could taste the salt air, which always made me feel at home, maybe because I had grown up on the ocean. I felt the breeze, which helped to maintain a perfect, balanced temperature.

Mother nature seems to have purposely made sand dunes as the ultimate comfort location. Where else can you sit on the ground and have the shape of the ground molded to your butt's shape?

As alive as my senses were and as tumultuous as the external world around me was, I felt an inner calm. My inner peace provided the space for my inner knowing. The usual cascading thoughts demanding center stage subsided to barely a whisper.

A deep, deep sense of gratitude swept over me. At first it seemed to be gratitude for being in this physical location. I was grateful for this but gratitude did not stop there.

At a deeper level, I was profoundly grateful for the blessings granted to me. God had blessed me by opening doors and providing opportunities to grow. I lingered on the sense of intense and joyous gratitude.

Then my gratitude shifted to the doors that had been opened for me. I reflected how I probably would not have seen these open doors twenty years ago.

Each open door revealed an opportunity to grow and serve. Variously the doors revealed teachers, books, remarkable people, projects, opportunities, and insights that represented the next steps on my journey. As the doors opened I increasingly "heard" insights that changed my life for the better. The more my intuition spoke, the better I heard. The better I heard, the more grateful and happy I became. Even the concept of "my journey" did not exist twenty years ago. Instead of a "journey" I thought in terms of a business career.

When I viewed the world through the lens of a business career, my vision was very narrow. From the perspective of a compass, I only saw about 10° either way. Today, from a different perspective, the breadth of my vision is rapidly reaching 360°.

Further reflection revealed that these were not just chance occasions. Each open door had perfect timing. Behind the door was exactly what I needed at that moment. Often this was not immediately obvious, but it became clear very quickly. The first sign was like an inner smile and sense of perfect comfort with where I found myself when I walked through the opened door. Logical understandings took longer to emerge but inevitably followed.

As I reflected on all the doors that opened for me over the last twenty years, I couldn't help but smile at the perfection that had unfolded. Each door opened in the right sequence with the right people there to help me and to be helped. For example, if my experience with Denise had not happened then I would not have gone deeper into MacLaine's work.... and certainly would not have so thoroughly embraced a channeled book like *Living With Joy* that helped to transform my life at the time. This insight created a "WOW!" sensation....and a few goose bumps.

I briefly reflected on the what might have been the first time my intuition spoke to me.....Denise?.....Marrying Patricia? Then I realized that it had been happening from even before my birth when my soul entered the union of sperm and egg. My entire life was full of events, people, and experiences that directed me to the next step on my journey. While from the perspective of this book, I have marked Denise and marrying Patricia as starting points of sorts, but it really encompasses my entire life. The reason I started this book with the two events noted as starting points is that they seem to represent the beginning of my spiritual journey.....they were a transition from the almost exclusive career focus to a broader focus that became the centerpiece of my life.

At first, the events in my life came slowly and one at a time. Gradually the pace increased. Towards the end of these twenty years multiple experiences occurred somewhat simultaneously. My experiences with José/Michael, healing, Sogyal, heart opening, Ageless Wisdom, and the quantum world were all going on about the same time over a period of several years. The more I learned the hungrier I became for more learning.

By this time the inkling that my intuition spoke had transformed into a strong belief that there was a purpose and a plan revealed in the insights and "messages." What had and was happening in my life made sense from the perspective of looking back at the series of events. Increasingly I could see how one learning experience created the conditions enabling another experience to unfold.

I sat and basked in the glow of all that had gone on so far. A sense of deep comfort and nurturing took center stage in my consciousness. I sat with all of this and just let it be.

This reverie was broken by my ego consciousness demanding center stage. It was like a switch had been turned on. All of a sudden it was there.

My ego consciousness reflected on what transpired in the last twenty years. These reflections held a mixture of pride and amazement. The first twenty years of conscious journey certainly had not been spent in a cave. There was abundant evidence in the external world of considerable activity.

I had written and published four books. I had researched and written a fifth that was now ready for publication.

I taught at a major university for six years. This was maybe the most remarkable and unexpected door that had opened.

I had started three successful companies.

I invented a new product that was now being commercialized.

I met and studied with one of the great masters on earth at this time.

I left a very high paying job with only one purpose: "To strengthen my relationship with God."

My loving relationship with my wife had grown steadily. My relationship with my two daughters also grew and represents a loving focal point of my life.

Viewed from the perspective of the outside world it was a busy and successful twenty years since my intuition first spoke. Seen from the perspective of my inner world, the storms and chaos gradually slowed down which is not to be confused with a consistently calm and peaceful world. Progress had been made. Much, much greater progress remains to be made.

Looking back, not one of the events of the last twenty years that I had just reviewed was a part of any specific plan that I made. I discovered that a journey is very different from a career. Prior to my journey years, my career years were filled with detailed objectives and plans. My journey years are characterized by being open to possibilities. The Universe would "speak" by opening a door. Being open to possibilities, I walked through the door. Even as possibilities and opportunities emerged into my vision, fixed plans and objectives were almost nonexistent. I continued to be in the moment and open to the possibilities represented by the opened door.

With that thought my ego consciousness turned to the future. I could not even imagine the next sixteen years of my journey being even half as eventful as the last sixteen years. I realized that imagining and planning for any specific life elements might only get in the way. Goals and objectives might only limit my ability to "hear" my intuition.

Suddenly I felt elated. There was no need or a burden to think things through or plan. The only plan I needed was to remain open to possibilities and be present when my intuition spoke. Excitement without attachment meant the future became an exhilarating range of possibilities.

I sat with this excitement. I felt more energized than I had ever been in my life. The combination of an exhilarating previous two decades and the uplifting possibilities of the next twenty years brought me to a new high.

Again, I basked in the glow of the moment.

I did not want it to end but the sun would set in another half hour or so. This realization broke the "spell" of the moment. I lifted myself up and began the next stage of my journey.

SEVENTEEN
CHAPTER

The Same Messages

Shortly after my time on the beach I realized that almost everything I read or heard the over the last few years was essentially different versions of the same messages.

This was no minor realization for me. I had been an incredibly voracious reader over the previous sixteen years. I have mentioned only a few of the highlights, but the total number of books exceeds 200. Some of the notable ones not mentioned so far include:

- Deepak Chopra's many books started with the mind and body connection and grew to spiritual teachings.
- Gary Zukav's books beginning with his book on quantum physics and continuing to books on the soul and spirituality.
- Dali Lama's books, both by him and about him. Also books by other Buddhist teachers, especially Rinpoche level teachers.
- *Conversations With God* series.

- Books about the Masters (*Living With the Himalayan Masters, Seven Years in Tibet* and *Life and Teaching of the Masters of the Far East* series, for example)
- Many books on quantum theory and its implications for us.
- The Ageless Wisdom series.

What I realized was that even from a somewhat big picture view there were essential truths. Different authors using different words might sound distinctive at first but even a modest amount of reflection revealed the different words communicated the same messages I had read from other authors. In part this was the influence of Ken Wilber who demonstrated in his seminal works how different writers from different cultures and different historical times with apparently different messages were really communicating parts of the same big picture. Even where there was apparent overlap, it was, for the most part, different dimensions that enriched the original idea.

But this realization went beyond the work of Ken Wilber for me. It was a deep inner sense. I gradually came to see that individual thinkers and authors communicated parts of the bigger picture. It appeared that those parts emerged into my life through open doors at exactly the time that I needed them to take the next steps on my journey. Over time I had collected many parts of the bigger picture.

I began to hunger for someone who saw not only the parts but also the big picture. I needed a teacher who could pull it all together in a way that made sense and, most importantly, helped me take the next big steps along my journey.

At the same time there was another element to my realization. At times I had read multiple books about the same subject, like the soul. While most of what they said about the soul was similar, the way in which they said it made a very big difference for me.

I realized that words have energy. From my study of quantum physics I knew I was an entity of energy. The words of certain authors were more synchronistic and therefore understandable for me than the words of other authors, even though they might be writing about the same topic. For me, there were some stunning examples. For example, one of the most popular books on the soul was *Care of the Soul* by Thomas Moore. Even though I had read many books on this topic and the book was easy-to-understand English, I struggled and ultimately learned almost nothing from the book. This is not a statement about the author but about how well the author's words and their associated energy were compatible with my own energy. Ultimately my ability to connect with the energy of the author through the words that he used determined the learning I achieved. The same is true for you as you read this book.

EIGHTEEN
CHAPTER

The One

I realized I was looking for the one teacher who could guide me for the rest of my life. While I wanted this and had established the intent to find that teacher, it certainly was not clear to me that wanting and intent would be enough.

I certainly had read many times "when the student is ready a teacher will emerge." Despite all of this I knew that I had done what I could do and now I needed to remain alert to the possibility of that one teacher I was looking for.

I did not have to wait too long.

As I read books of interest, I would often find the author referring to a teacher, author, or another book and this would lead me to learn more. This is how I found Paramahansa Yogananda.

I was reading a book by Susan Smith Jones who had some very interesting books on nutrition (her specialty as a professor at UCLA) and spirituality. In it she mentioned that Paramahansa Yogananda was her spiritual teacher. My intuition spoke.

Even at this first introduction, I had an inkling of possibilities. I searched Amazon and discovered that his major book is *An Autobiography of a Yogi*. Remarkably, for all of the year 2000 it was the number one selling spirituality book on Amazon, which is amazing considering that he passed in 1952.

Other than Susan's brief reference to him, my learning about who he was did not begin until I read this book. The book got my attention. Not only is his life remarkable but also I found a very strong connection with the "energy" of the book. It is almost like the words sang a beautiful and enticing song that quickly became one of my favorites.

I really connected with a crucial part of his life's mission which was to bring together Western and Eastern spirituality. He was given this mission by Mahavatar Babaji, a legendary master of masters. His mission struck a very powerful chord for me since I saw artificial divides between spiritual traditions and between spirituality and science. Here was a great person showing how they were all one. When you enter a Self Realization Fellowship (SRF) temple or other facility you see prominent pictures of Jesus and Krishna....underscoring the unity of East and West.

I learned that he founded the Self Realization Fellowship. This was another very strong connection for me since I was much more into individual study and practice than I was into group efforts. As I explored their web site, I learned that I could subscribe to weekly lessons written by Paramahansa Yogananda. When I started receiving them, I was struck by their practical advice on a wide range of topics ranging from nutrition to healing to advanced spiritual practices. The lessons were sequenced to build on each other every week and the lessons unfolded over about three years. This was exactly what I needed and my spiritual progress leapt forward.

In addition to the lessons, I explored more about his life and who he was. I talked with brothers in the Fellowship and studied what others had written about him. From both external and internal sources (with the latter being much more influential) I knew that he was a God realized being. He had progressed along the human evolutionary path and "graduated" from the human kingdom. In the real and full sense of the word he became enlightened (today this is an often misused and misunderstood word).....he was an avatar....a divine incarnation confirmed by many masters. He had returned to human form to help others along the journey that he had completed. This excerpt from his poetry (*Man's Eternal Quest*) brings a special dimension to his return to help others.

> I went to ply my boat, many times,
> Across the gulf-after-death,
> And return to earth's shores from my house in Heaven.
> I want to load my boat
> With those waiting, thirsty ones who are left behind,
> And carry them by the opal pool of iridescent joy
> Where my Father distributes
> His all-desire-quenching liquid peace.

Other spiritual traditions and teachers have the same insight.... Buddhists call it the Bodhisattva vow, for example.

The information in the preceding paragraph that Yogananda is a God realized being might be viewed with skepticism my many/most who read this...as it should be. You should not accept information like this based solely on external sources....like me. Rather, you should conduct your own exploration and most importantly do the inner work necessary to develop some meaningful and trusted level of inner knowing.

After a few months, I became aware of two critical insights that have profoundly influenced my life ever since. First, I realized that the hunger mentioned earlier had been satiated with the emergence of my guru for life, Paramahansa Yogananda. This relationship grew into a deep love for him.

Second, as a God realized being I knew that God spoke through him. As he said, "If we allow our will to be led by the wisdom of a master, whose will is in tune with the God's, the master then seeks to guide our will in such a way that we travel swiftly on the road back to divinity." His teachings came from God...and as I shared earlier, Paramahansa Yogananda said, "God doesn't talk to man direct, but uses the channel of a guru and his teachings" and "It is His spirit that talks to you through me." In a separate quote he said, "A true guru is the servant of God, carrying out His plan for your liberation."

Beautifully his teachings were in their original English form, un-translated and unchanged by other humans. And the energy of his words resonated strongly with me. I felt an incredibly strong connection and felt I could see with clarity most of his teachings.

God spoke and I was intoxicated in His love.

Yogananda is my guru. I had had many teachers…Sogyal was one of the greatest…but never a guru before. I define a guru as someone I deeply love and trust with all aspects of my spiritual development. Yogananda's teachings are comprehensive and at the highest possible level…simply he had it all for me.

Later in my relationship with him I discovered this advice from him that resonated strongly with my own experience.

> "In the beginning of one's spiritual search, it is wise to compare various spiritual paths and teachers. But when you find the real guru destined for you, the one whose teachings can lead you to the Divine Goal, then restless searching should cease. A spiritually thirsty person should not go on indefinitely seeking new wells; rather he should go to the best well and drink daily of its living waters."

Since choosing Yogananda as my guru, my spiritual progress has been dramatic compared to the progress I made via very conscious efforts prior to this relationship. This progress traces to a variety of insights and new methods of which there are three major ones.

First, the spiritual practices he teaches have deepened and accelerated my progress towards self-realization (still a long, long way off for me!). In the lessons, he unfolds a building series of meditation practice that deepen the meditative experience. Generally speaking, he teaches powerful focal points in combination with a mantra. He later builds on this practice with a process of intense focus on hearing subtle sacred sounds. This building process culminates in the teaching of Kriya yoga. (Different teachers translate "Yoga" in different ways, but I have always identified with the definition of "union with God.") Kriya is an exceptionally powerful spiritual practice. In about thirty minutes of Kriya one can make about 100 years of spiritual progress (100 years of using spiritual practices other than Kriya). Qualifying for Kriya lessons and then initiation requires extensive practice and experience with all of the previous forms of spiritual practices taught by him. I needed to have my practices reviewed and approved by a monk of the Fellowship before I could receive the lesson and then initiation.

These spiritual practices now constitute the major focus of every day for me. I spend about two hours per day meditating, practicing Kriya, praying, and studying his lessons.

Second, he left us with an exceptionally broad, deep, and diverse set of lessons and writings. As mentioned previously, what is so refreshing and helpful about these works are they are all in the original English. So many of the other major spiritual teachings, like the Christian Bible, are not in their original form. They have been edited and translated/interpreted many times. Some of these efforts have been well intended but some of them have been self-serving. All of the efforts to understand the meaning of these other major spiritual teachings required translations that were conducted by people who did not have the spiritual development of the original authors. They, therefore, could not be expected to fully understand the importance and meaning of the original teachings. We do not face that problem with Yogananda's teachings....although we do face the challenge of personal interpretation and understanding.

I have already mentioned the almost three years worth of introductory lessons available to all members of the Self Realization Fellowship. Their value and assistance is extraordinary.

Beyond these writings, he provides powerfully insightful commentary on major parts of the Christian Bible. His two volumes of commentary made this extraordinary sacred text understandable to me for the first time. I was able to read an interpretation of the Christian Bible written by a person with equal spiritual development to the original authors. Yogananda's exceptional ability with the English-language revealed profound meanings that were simply stated.

He did the same thing for the *Bhagavad-Gita, the Royal Science of God Realization.* In two volumes he provides a new translation and commentary that has made this sacred text a core part of my daily study. It is an extraordinarily comprehensive set of literal teachings that, for me, provide all I could ever need along the path to self-realization.

He taught me an extraordinarily new method of study. Through my academic and business work my method of study focused on pouring through quantities of writing and analysis. His message shifted me from quantity to quality. Now my daily study often focuses on one sentence, one paragraph, or one page. I was now reading to assimilate. I was now reading to intuitively "get" meaning I could feel. This new method was so powerful that many times I felt the very small section I was reading could be the only insight I might need for the balance of my life. If I could only learn to live the meaning of the small portion, I could see my life being transformed.

Some sections of the Gita I often read, then go back and reread, then go back and reread some more and continuing to do this for months at a time. For example, in one section he enumerates the twenty-six soul qualities that make a man God-like. This is an example of a section that I have reread for months at a time. I read about one quality per day and really try to get its full meaning. Each time I reread a section I am surprised about how much additional meaning I gain.

As my relationship with Yogananda grew, I realized that I could listen to God anytime by reading Yogananda's words. Since Yogananda is a God realized being, I knew that God spoke through Yogananda. This was not my personal conclusion alone since previous readings and studies had consistently revealed that over time a very few God realized beings returned to earth with lessons and insights from God. I knew that I needed to be cautious about this since there is no shortage of preachers claiming to talk to God and to speak for God. The difference between them and Yogananda was startling and profound, making the knowing that Yogananda spoke for God and easy conclusion for me to reach.

It was easy to reach because of all the prior work I had done. For example, I had read over 200 books, many by relatively highly evolved humans. I had studied personally with Sogyal Rinpoche and knew from his example what a highly evolved person was like....but a person who stated clearly that he was not enlightened; was not a God realized being. I knew Yogananda was more. I knew that other highly evolved beings spoke openly that he was an avatar or God realized being. Most importantly for me my inner knowing had been developed enough through many years of mediation that I had grown to recognize and respect it. All of my inner knowing confirmed his position as a God realized being.

It will not be so easy for many of you reading this....and that is as it should be. You have heard of preachers and various "holy" people who claim that God speaks directly to them. I have also heard this but my experience is that they speak from very narrow and usually self-serving perspectives. Typically they want my loyalty and money. With Yogananda I was never asked for money or loyalty....but I choose to give it of my own free will.

Please do not take my word that Yogananda was a God realized being whose words and teachings come from God to us. Please do the work necessary to broaden your understandings of the spiritual world and the inner work to awaken your inner knowing to the point that it becomes a trusted source of ultimate knowing for you.

I am so, so deeply grateful for the opportunity to totally embrace with deep devotion my love and commitment to Yogananda as my guru for life. I discovered the truth of statements that "one may have many teachers, that only one guru."

I no longer needed to rely only on life events as the major source for God's lessons. While life events continue to play a significant role for incremental learning, my learning focal point now and for the rest of my life is on Yogananda's teachings.

With my shift from searching to guru dedication, my wisdom inspired life jumped into a much high pace. My intuition was functioning every day. Wisdom poured into my life. As it did, I continued to recognize the very, very modest progress I had made relative to what lay ahead of me. From this insight there is not one ounce of discouragement. There is only excitement of the wisdom inspired life that is on a road that is right in front of me.

NINTEEN
CHAPTER

Making A Difference

Yogananda made a profound real world difference in my life.

The richness and depth of his teachings are uplifting and inspiring to me. I am highly motivated to change my life for the better with his help. He notes that the achievement of self-realization or enlightenment is 25% the result of the individual's effort, 25% the result of a guru's blessing and help, and 50% the blessing of God. I am deeply committed to carrying my full share of responsibility on this journey.

His teachings represented the first time since *Living With Joy* that I had a blueprint for fundamentally changing my life. While I dramatically expanded my understanding of spirituality in the world around me, I gleaned from all of his teachings three insights that work every day to move me further along on the journey to self-realization. At heart I am a very practical person that means that theory and speculation have very limited value for me. I only adopted insights from a God realized teacher that resonated with my inner knowing as truth. It is not that others were not valuable but that these were the ones most helpful to me based on where I am on the journey now.

Insight #1: Regarding GOD....

...GOD is....nay, GOD.

That is all we need to know to propel lifetimes of journeys.

Insight #2: Meditation and yoga

Yogananda: "By meditation we connect the little joy of the soul to the vast joy of the Spirit. Meditation should not be confused with ordinary concentration.... Meditation is that special form of concentration in which the attention has been liberated from restlessness and is focused on God. Meditation, therefore, is concentration used to know God."

The spiritual traditions indicate that there are several paths to the achievement of self-realization. For example, there are the paths of devotion and the discriminating mind. The former involves activities like extensive prayer, performing of rituals, and sacrifice that can possibly include renunciation. The latter can involve activities like the proactive application of spiritual principles in making decisions and intensive study of Scripture.

The wisdom traditions are also clear that the fastest path to self-realization is built on an intensive, committed, and scientific practice of meditation. My practice of meditation started about twenty years ago with ten minutes spent immediately after waking up in the morning. As I write this book, my spiritual practice every day lasts for about two hours, typically in two one-hour sessions. In these sessions there is prayer and study of sacred texts prior to meditation and Kriya practice. While my business often includes extensive travel, almost every non-travel day includes the two hours of practice, which may be reduced to one hour on travel days. My spiritual practice is the highest priority every day.

I quickly learned that the meditative methods and focus were far more important than the amount of time. Prior to Yogananda's teachings my primary focus was on a simple mantra, repeating the word "love." I arrived at this method after studying and learning how exquisitely simple the various meditative methods were. They all involved a fairly simple focal point: a mantra, observing the breath, and/or chakra focus. After brief experimentation I chose my mantra and it proved to be somewhat effective in calming what appeared to be a never-ending restlessness.

Looking back I am somewhat surprised that I maintained an every day meditation practice when I experienced so little apparent progress. Restlessness, not peace and calm, dominated every meditation session. Progress was difficult to detect since restlessness remained high and I did not experience any breakthrough or spiritual phenomenon. Even my best meditation experiences in the early years were small positive experiences that appeared to be hardly noteworthy.

Yogananda's encouragement and wisdom kept on the path....counsel like....

"The most distractive shaft of *maya*-delusion is unwillingness to meditate, for by this attitude one prevents himself from tuning in with God and Guru." "The more sweetening you put in water, the sweeter it becomes. Likewise, the longer you meditate intensely, the greater will be your spiritual advancement."

"What joy awaits discovery in the silence behind the portals of your mind no human tongue can tell. But you must convince yourself; you must meditate and create that environment."

Insight #3: Teachers and Guru

Along my spiritual journey teachers and ultimately a guru played critical roles. The vast majority of us are unprepared for such a journey when the first inklings emerge in our consciousness. Even those experienced in a specific religious tradition may have only a very narrow path outlined for them that may not be the best match for their needs.

When the first inklings appear consider this a sign that your curiosity has been ignited. It is time to act. Act by putting yourself in a spiritual, religious, metaphysical, and/or personal growth environment. Go to a bookstore and just trust your instincts about what book interest you most. Google the Internet and trust those same instincts. Purchase some magazines like EnlightenmentNext, which contain provocative articles and many advertisements for spiritual teachers and books. Trust what you're attracted to.

Engage! Read with deep interest. When something truly intrigues you, go deeper. Go deeper by reading small sections and reflecting on their meaning, especially their personal meaning. "Feel" the meaning. Let it sink in.

If the subject interests you, then find another book by the same author or one on the same subject by a different author. When one book refers to new subject matter that captures your attention, go to Amazon and order it. Trust that what grabs your attention is meant to be.

As you move along your spiritual journey, look for opportunities to be in the presence of advanced teachers. Be careful. Many people who present themselves as "advanced" are really only advanced in the art of collecting your money. Again, you need to trust your inner guidance system.

Humility and joy are hallmarks of an advanced teacher. Spend some time with a Buddhist Rinpoche. Bask in their energy. Feel their presence. Turn your attention inward.

You may have a teacher for a day or years. At some point you may discover you have learned what they have to teach and are living in your life. It's time to move on to the next teacher. But before doing so take a moment to express your gratitude.

A series of teachers emerge along the journey. When you are aware and present, you connect with just the right teacher for you at this exact place in your journey. Engage. Learn. Live.

Most teachers have a partial understanding that is usually drawn from their own journey. These parts are often exactly the parts we need at a point in time. Teachers are most often specialists. They have part of the "puzzle."

At some point you may or may not be ready for a guru. A guru has many parts of the "puzzle." The most advanced have all the parts. There are very few of these on the earth today or who have been on the earth in the last couple of thousand years. They are often referred to as avatars or divine incarnations. These are people who have "graduated" from the human experience by progressing through the three higher states of consciousness, higher than only the waking and subconscious states that the vast majority of us experience. Yogananda is an acknowledged divine incarnation.

When you fully embrace your guru, they are the only teacher you need. This is not because I said so, but because they fulfill all of your needs. Loyalty is willingly given. A bond is formed for this and probably many future lifetimes.

A brief note of caution is necessary. There are teachers who claim to be "enlightened" and they, in my experience and opinion, do so with some very loose definitions of what that keyword means. For many "enlightened" means that they had an epiphany into the spiritual world. Unfortunately, epiphanies, no matter how enlightening they may feel, do not qualify per most definitions of "enlightened." There are some very spiritually advanced beings like Sogyal Rinpoche who openly say they are not enlightened. The bar for enlightenment is VERY high.

In my experience enlightened is synonymous with self-realization. It is what we experience when we progress from subconscious and waking conscious experiences to super consciousness, Christ consciousness, and ultimately cosmic consciousness. In the language of the Ageless Wisdom, it is when we complete the third, fourth, and fifth initiations. The combination of both of these cycles means that we "graduate" from the human kingdom into the next kingdom. We become God realized beings. That is true enlightenment.

When you choose a guru, your journey's pace picks up and the vast unknown of the spiritual journey reveals itself to your inner wisdom. Enjoy the ride!

TWENTY
CHAPTER

Karma....Tough But An Opportunity

Karma stinks!

This is especially true for negative karma and especially in the early stages.

You may recall from an earlier chapter that karma is all about consequences from our actions. Every action we take has consequences. When we perform a negative action, an action that violates spiritual laws like stealing from others, we will experience the consequences of that action in the future. The "future" can be in this lifetime or in a future lifetime. Often the consequences can be as literal as the causal event. For example, when it comes time to experience the consequences of stealing from others, we will experience others stealing from us.

Yogananda has this perspective, "By the divine decree of the cosmic law of karma, cause-and-effect, every human being is born with propensities that are good, evil, or activating, according to the nature of his response, in a previous incarnation, to the three cosmic qualities. Thus every individual comes into this world with a specific self-created temperament, and is predisposed to certain habits and moods, the inherited result of oft repeated actions in a former life."

Shortly after finishing the previous chapter, I experienced an intense negative karma event for about fifteen months. While the details of this particular event are not relevant for here, my experience with the event is relevant.

What I find so interesting is that before the triggering event, I prepared more for this single event than any other one I can recall in recent times. By prepare I mean getting perspective and advice from several other people. My goal was to do the right thing, the right way. I thought I had done an exceptional job preparing for the event that triggered significant negative karmic consequences for me.

I know at a very deep level from my spiritual teachings and experiences that karmic events are teaching and learning opportunities. The deep challenge for me is that often until a karmic event has concluded it is very difficult for me to determine what I am supposed to learn. This is especially in the early stages where there is pain and confusion. It is not fun!

This event for me involved deep psychological and emotional pain. At times the emotional pain was so intense that it virtually immobilized me. Even when it was not intense, it seemed to pervade almost every moment of my life. It was like a dark cloud that followed me around. I had never experienced anything like this. Its pervasiveness and intensity seemed so way out of proportion to the event itself. The event is one that many people face and while it can be emotionally upsetting, it is seldom as intense and pervasive as I experienced.

This also had physiological consequences. My energy level was consistently lower than normal. During moments of emotional intensity, there was also physical discomfort. With my doctor's assistance, I experimented with some pharmaceutical options. With one occasional exception, they were not very helpful and I discontinued them after a short period of time.

And the fact that I was experiencing all this over a particular event made absolutely no sense to me. My reaction was, so I thought, far more intense than the facts warranted. So much for facts! The very irrationality compounded the conundrum.

I sought counseling. It provided some modest benefits. It defused some of the pain.

All of this apparent irrationality told me at a very deep level this was karmic in origin. Very spiritually developed humans can access the actual causes of a karmic event in their life, but I am very far from being one of those people. As a result, I could not easily connect with the cause and, more importantly, what I was supposed to learn from all of this.

I researched and read books. Eckhart Towle's *The Power of Now* provided some helpful advice. Specifically, he recommends observing the pain in your body. I came to call this my "emotional pain body" that I observed. The process of observing changes both perspective and relationship with the pain. These changes enabled me to fairly quickly and easily release the most intense emotional pain. While effective, it provided short-term benefits. The pain would recur and the process repeated. At least there was pain reduction that previous methods had not provided.

Not surprisingly, the spiritual solutions were the ones I pursued most vigorously. There were intense periods of meditation. I read and reread and reread Yogananda's advice. I had conversations with leaders in the Fellowship.

Most importantly for me, I began a very intense one-way conversation with God. I often had several one-way conversations a day. Some of this was a blatant request for help. Most of my communication was seeking understanding, especially what I was supposed to learn from the event.

Progress was very slow as proven by the fifteen months required to acquire the necessary learning. It was an experience almost unlike any other one I had experienced previously in my life. It was a dark cloud that was there when I woke up in the morning, followed me around during the day, and went to bed with me at night. It hurt. It diminished me. It went well beyond anything logical which made it mysterious and frustrating.

At the time I am writing this, I am less than one year away from its conclusion. To be fair there is still a bit of mystery about all of this. One thing is clear. The one-way frequent conversations I began with God have become a regular part of my life. This has enriched my life by deepening my connection. My journey has moved to a more personal relationship from one that was more distant. Increasingly I ask the question, "What would God do?" The answer is always simple and clear. My ego often injects its two cents but is less and less likely to rule the moment.

For this I am deeply grateful.

To Be Continued......

For more than 20 years I have had the privilege of living an increasingly wisdom inspired life. It has been a radical change from the knowledge and logic dominated life that preceded it.

While it may appear that there are similarities between wisdom and knowledge defined life, the differences are profound. The similarities are that there can be reading a book or listening to a speaker. This would seem to have, based on the definitions that I presented earlier, a knowledge profile since the information is coming in from external sources. The difference is what happens with the inputs. With the lower or knowledge mind, the inputs are processed by logic and emotions. With the upper or wisdom mind, the inputs are processed by our intuition.

With the wisdom mind, the inner knowing is difficult to describe, but I refer to it as inputs that resonate as a deep and abiding truth. I use the word resonate because of the energy component of the experience. The inner knowing is that the input's energy is totally consistent with the essence of who I really am. For me, there is no stronger experience of truth.

MY WISDOM INSPIRED LIFE

This lifetime is not ready to conclude. I continue to be a work in progress. So far my life has been as Albert Camus said, "Life is a sum of all our choices."

Maybe there will be a time when I write a subsequent book about the next chapters in my journey. Based on my current experiences, there is no shortage of material for a potential next book.

Some provocative developments are currently underway and not well understood.

The last year, I have been openly and frequently talking to God. Mostly it is a one-way conversation. The few times I feel it is a two-way conversation is when I experience an energy shift as a direct and immediate result of talking to God. It seems like it's very much the right thing to do.

I have faced one of the most emotionally challenging experiences of my life. It seems to be in my life to teach me about handling emotions under very trying circumstances. It is also having some very intriguing spiritual dimensions.

There is an emerging sense that things are beginning to move faster and faster. At this point, I'm not sure what that's all about.

And what I am most curious about is to discover why I am writing and publishing this book. It started as a self-exploratory learning experience, which is how most of my books have started. But it seems to have turned into something more. What that "more" is I am intensely curious to discover.

While I can see that this book is a natural next step given my previous steps, it's not clear what future steps it will lead to.......but that is the nature of these things. When you're in the middle of a significant life event (which this book may or may not be), it is best to be totally present since spending time on the future speculation is a fool's folly.

My focus as I write this book is on bringing my ego under the control of my soul. My ego is my biggest "enemy." Its focus on "I" is at the heart of every challenge and problem I face. Its power and domination in my consciousness inspires both awe and frustration. It is the most formidable challenge and barrier to making the spiritual and wisdom progress I so deeply know to be right. Again, meditation is the "weapon" of choice in this battle. Playing a supporting role are resources and practices like prayer, study of Scripture, being present, and creating a discriminating logical and emotional being.

Changing focus, here are some quick concluding thoughts on how you might apply the fundamentals of my experience to your life.

- Attempt to see the big picture of your life so far. Consider writing down the sequence of major events in your life.
- Look for connections between events. For example, if event A had not occurred then is it highly unlikely that event B would've occurred? Expand your view to see additional linkages. For example, from my experience you know that if the Denise experience had not occurred, then the Shirley Maclaine experience probably would not occurred, and the *Living with Joy* seminal event probably would not have occurred.
- Remember everything that has happened so far in your life has happened for a reason. As you look at the linkages in your life, where are they headed? Have any of these events changed or expanded your worldview paradigm of how things work? Recall how my very strong left brain orientation to the world fundamentally changed to a more expansive set of left-brain, right brain, and higher consciousness capabilities to interact with the world around me.
- How does seeing the big picture of your life and some of the basic directions your life is headed change/influence your view of the present and future? Are you more open to new possibilities? Are you more proactively curious to learn more? Does your life take on a greater sense of purpose and direction? How do you feel about all this?

Having a better understanding of your life can make it more comfortable and give you more confidence. Having a clearer sense of purpose and direction for your life, can be an exquisitely powerful force leading to greater happiness and success.

Enjoy!

Feel free to connect with me at haasnoot@cox.net.

To be continued...........

APPENDIX A

Suggested Reading

Paramahansa Yogananda

- *Autobiography of a Yogi*
- *Bhagavad-Gita, the Royal Science of God Realization*
- *The Second Coming of Christ*
- *The Law of Success*
- *How to Be Happy All the Time.*
- *Man's Eternal Quest.*

Sogyal Rinpoche: *The Tibetan Book of Living and Dying.*
Sanaya Roman:
- *Living with Joy.*
- *Personal Power through Awareness*
- *Spiritual Growth. Being Your Higher Self.*

Jose Stevens
- *Earth to Tao*
- *Tao To Earth*

The Ageless Wisdom: Published by Lucis Publishing Company.
 Any Book by the Dalai Lama.
The Conversations with God Series.
Eckhart Tolle: *The Power of Now*.

[i] Ponder on This, page 423

[ii] Ponder on This, page 424

[iii] Ibit, page 223

[iv] Ibit, page 223

[v] Ibit, page 223

www.ingramcontent.com/pod-product-compliance
Lightning Source LLC
Chambersburg PA
CBHW061731020426
42331CB00006B/1192